DICTIONARY *of*

LITURGY &
WORSHIP

BRETT SCOTT PROVANCE

IVP Academic
An imprint of InterVarsity Press
Downers Grove, Illinois

InterVarsity Press
P.O. Box 1400,
Downers Grove, IL 60515-1426
World Wide Web: www.ivpress.com
E-mail: email@ivpress.com

InterVarsity Press® is the book-publishing division of InterVarsity Christian Fellowship/
USA®, a student movement active on campus at hundreds of universities, colleges and schools
of nursing in the United States of America, and a member movement of the International
Fellowship of Evangelical Students. For information about local and regional activities, write
Public Relations Dept., InterVarsity Christian Fellowship/USA, 6400 Schroeder Rd., P.O.
Box 7895, Madison, WI 53707-7895, or visit the IVCF website at <www.intervarsity.org>.

Scripture quotations, unless otherwise noted, are from the New Revised Standard Version
of the Bible, copyright 1989 by the Division of Christian Education of the National Council
of the Churches of Christ in the USA. Used by permission. All rights reserved.

Design: Cindy Kiple

Images: Roberta Polfus

ISBN 978-0-8308-2707-7

Printed in the United States of America ∞

Library of Congress Cataloging-in-Publication Data

Provance, Brett S. (Brett Scott), 1963-
  Pocket dictionary of liturgy and worship / Brett Scott Provance.
    p. cm.
  Includes bibliographical references.
  ISBN 978-0-8308-2707-7 (pbk.: alk. paper)
  1. Liturgy—Dictionaries. 2. Worship—Dictionaries. I. Title.
  BV173.P76 2009
  264.003—dc22

                                                                    2009026592

P   20   19   18   17   16   15   14   13   12   11   10   9   8   7   6   5   4   3   2   1

Y   25   24   23   22   21   20   19   18   17   16   15   14   13   12   11   10   09

Preface

THIS *POCKET DICTIONARY* WAS WRITTEN IN the interest of the continuing and growing attention given to the structure and content of Christian worship. The purpose of this dictionary is first and foremost to provide quick information concerning Christian corporate worship.

Beyond this goal, the dictionary helps to

- demystify liturgical terms
- complement biblical and theological studies by providing copious references, both to establish the biblical basis or rationale of elements in corporate worship and to aid in the study of the historical interplay of Scripture and liturgy
- increase sensitivity to liturgical *meanings* through an interdisciplinary approach, that is, not just through written texts, but also through (e.g.) art and architecture
- inform contemporary Christians of the longer historical tradition (Evangelicals are attuned to the *theological* categories and developments of Christian history but less so, until recent years, to the *liturgies* in Christian history.)

ABOUT THE ENTRIES

Traditional Christian corporate worship revolves around two regular services, namely the Sunday service and the Daily Office. It is these two services that are a specific focus of this *Pocket Dictionary*, as most of what is involved in Christian liturgy and worship is part of these two services. Worship or devotional life of a more individual interest is only incidental to this work.

Beyond focusing on the two services of Christian corporate worship, the *Pocket Dictionary* addresses the liturgical year and the traditional time parameters of the Christian community intertwining with the life of individual Christians in the world (daily, seasonally, yearly, lifespan), thus enhancing sensitivity to this particular aspect of Christian worship.

A dictionary this size is limited in what and whom it covers. Certain people and places were selected because they were significantly innovative or representative. Scriptural references and allusions in the entries suggest similar themes (analogy), perhaps a common source for consideration (homology) but not necessarily historical derivation (genealogy). Singular contributions to information within an entry are noted by the author's name in parentheses (with bibliographical information in the bibliography).

As far as liturgical forms given in some entries, this dictionary does not make any pretense of giving the only "right" or "pure" form of a Christian rite. Not only is Christianity quite diverse on certain issues (a synchronic aspect), but historical ambiguity at times must also be admitted (a diachronic aspect). Variations abound, even in the ancient churches, though there are remarkable similarities in general. What is presented here are generalizations that are representative of a number of traditions in a number of details, but not any one tradition in particular (unless so stated). Generalizations, yes, but by these the student will be better equipped to deal with differences in particulars (indeed, this *Pocket Dictionary* is intended as an aid and impetus to further study). The liturgical traditions are the ever-evolving expressions of the church concerning God's work in creation and salvation, the appropriate responses of the redeemed.

THE PSALMS

The Hebrew text of the Old Testament and the Greek translation of the Old Testament (the Septuagint) differ in the enumeration of the Psalms. Protestant Bibles, and some Roman Catholic Bibles, follow the Hebrew text with little variation. The Orthodox Church uses the Septuagint enumeration. In this *Dictionary*, references to the Psalms follow the Hebrew (and thus Protestant) enumeration. When, however, two numbers for a Psalm are given—for example, Ps 141 (140)—the first number is that of the Hebrew Bible and the second number in parentheses is that of the Septuagint. These different enumerations should be kept in mind even within academic contexts in that some scholars use the Septuagint numbering. Table A sets out the corresponding enumeration schemes.

Table A. Numbering of Psalms Compared

	Hebrew Bible/Protestant	Septuagint (LXX)/Orthodox
Psalms	1–8	1–8
	9–10	9
	11–113	10–112
	114–115	113
	116:1-9	114
	116:10-19	115
	117–146	116–145
	147.1-11	146
	147:12-20	147
	148–150	148–150

I wish to express gratitude to a number of persons for their kind suggestions in the process of compiling this dictionary, namely, Kim Riddlebarger, Beverly Howard, Rick Ritchie and Patty Broesamle, and especially Dan Reid of IVP for his editorial recommendations. I also wish to thank Mitchell Provance for the illustration in the appendix.

Abbreviations

1 Clem.	*1 Clement* (written in Rome c. 96)
ABCP	Anglican *Book of Common Prayer* (Church of England)
AC	Anglican Communion
Ap. Trad.	*Apostolic Tradition* (chapter divisions are those of the edition by Bradshaw, Johnson and Phillips)
Aram.	Aramaic
Art. Rel.	[The Thirty-Nine] Articles of Religion (Church of England)
Aug. Conf.	Augsburg Confession (Lutheran)
Barn.	*Barnabas*
BCP	The *Book of Common Prayer* in general, any number of editions
BF&M	Baptist Faith and Message (Southern Baptist Convention)
c.	*circa*, around, about
CCC	*Catechism of the Catholic Church*
CW	*Common Worship* (Church of England)
Cyr., *Myst. Cat.*	Cyril of Jerusalem's *Mystagogical Catecheses* (mid-fourth century)
Cyr., *Procatech.*	Cyril of Jerusalem's *Procatechesis* (mid-fourth century)
Did.	*Didache*
EBCP	Episcopal *Book of Common Prayer* (1979 edition) used by the Protestant Episcopal Church in the United States of America
EC	The Eastern churches, generally the Greco-Russian Orthodox churches, but also including the Syrian and Coptic churches, et al.
e.g.	*exempli gratia*, for example
Eng.	English
f.	feminine
F&O	Faith and Order papers of the World Council of Churches
fl.	flourished
Fr.	French

Ger.	German
Germ.	Germanus's *On the Divine Liturgy*
Gk.	Greek
Heb.	Hebrew
Heid. Cat.	Heidelberg Catechism (Reformed)
Herm., *Sim.*	Shepherd of Hermas, *Similitude*
i.e.	*id est*, that is to say, namely
Ign.	Ignatius of Antioch's letters (c. 110), e.g., *To the Ephesians*
Iren., *Haer.*	Irenaeus, *Adversus haereses* (Eng. *Against Heresies*)
Justin, *1 Apol.*	Justin Martyr, *First Apology* (to Emperor Antoninus Pius, reign 138-161)
Justin, *Dial.*	Justin Martyr, *Dialogue with Trypho*
Lat.	Latin
LC	Lutheran church
LG	*Lumen Gentium* (Dogmatic Constitution on the Church, Vatican II document)
LXX	Septuagint
NT	New Testament
OC	Orthodox Church
OT	Old Testament
P&RC	Presbyterian and Reformed churches
pl.	plural
PGM	*Papyri Graecae Magicae: Die griechischen Zauberpapyri* (ed. Karl Preisendanz, 1973)
RC	Roman Catholic Church
RR	Radical Reformation (Anabaptist groups, e.g., Mennonites, or those influenced by the Anabaptists, e.g., various Brethren groups)
SC	*Sacrosanctum concilium* (Constitution on the Sacred Liturgy, Vatican II document)
Sm. Cat.	Small Catechism of Martin Luther
Tert.	Tertullian: *Apologeticus* (Eng. *Apology*); *De baptismo* (Eng. *Baptism*); *De oratione* (Eng. *Prayer*)
WC	Western church(es), especially the Roman Catholic, Anglican/Episcopal, Lutheran, Presbyterian, Reformed and Methodist
West. Conf.	Westminster Confession of Faith (Presbyterian)

Cross-references

This pocket dictionary is cross-referenced using the following system:

An asterisk (*) before a word or phrase indicates that an entry on that topic, similarly worded, appears elsewhere in the book.

A *see*, followed by a subject and placed in parentheses, may be used instead of an asterisk to direct readers to a relevant entry.

See also references at the end of entries direct readers to related topics.

An alphabetized entry title with no definition is followed by *See* and the name of the entry under which the definition will be found.

A

a cappella. Italian for music "in the chapel manner," i.e., human voice only (e.g., *plainsong). Some Protestant churches today downplay the use of musical instruments in public worship.

abbey. A *monastery, headed by an *abbot or abbess.

abbot, abbess. From Aramaic (*ʾabbāʾ*) for "father," the head of a *monastery or *abbey. If an abbey consists of *nuns, the head nun is called an *abbess*.

Aberkios Inscription. One of the earliest extant Christian inscriptions (late second century), found in the vicinity of ancient Hierapolis in present-day Turkey. The inscription (written in Greek, partially restored from other sources) is a funerary memorial for *Bishop Aberkios of Hierapolis and speaks the language of early Christian *symbolism. For example, Aberkios identifies himself as a disciple of the Holy Shepherd (*see* Good Shepherd) and, along with friends (Gk. *philoi*), Faith served him as nourishment a *fish (*see* ΙΧΘΥΣ) seized by a pure *virgin, pleasant (Gk. *chrēstos*) *wine and *bread. Thus the inscription shares imagery with Roman Christian *catacomb art, in other words, a banquet of fish and loaves (cf. the feeding stories of Mk 6:32-44; 8:1-9).

ablution. A ritual or ceremonial washing.

absolution. Derived from Latin *absolvo*, "to release"; follows *confession of sin in liturgies. It is the *priest's or *minister's speech-act of forgiving the congregation of their sins, due to the recognized position of the priest (based on Mt 16:18-19; Jn 20:23). In some churches absolution merely means that the minister is qualified to remind and comfort the congregation that their sins are forgiven on account of Christ's work (i.e., a simple *declaration of forgiveness).

abstinence. The act of abstaining or forbidding oneself certain bodily satisfactions, such as food, drink, sex or sleep. Abstinence is a part of Christian spirituality (e.g., Acts 21:9; *see* asceticism), and some abstentions are encouraged in the NT for religious reasons (e.g., 1 Cor 7:5; 8:1-13). Traditionally, abstaining from eating before partaking of the *Eucharist has been encouraged. *Advent and *Lent are historically periods of abstinence. *See also* fast.

acclamation. The congregation's vocalized assent, for example, following the Gospel *reading in the RC *Liturgy of the Word.

acolyte. A person who assists with the liturgy (Gk. *akolouthos*, "follower"). The position is sometimes filled by a youth, in which case it is synonymous with *altar boy*, though it is now common for girls to serve as acolytes as well.

Advent. The calendrical period in the WC incorporating the four *Sundays preceding *Christmas Day, anticipating the coming (Lat. *adventus*) of Jesus Christ. The first week of Advent begins with the Sunday nearest the Feast of St. *Andrew (Nov. 30), that first Advent Sunday also beginning the WC *liturgical year. The season dates from the fifth or sixth century. Historically it is a period characterized by an attitude of repentance (though now downplayed) and anticipation, with preaching focused on the prophetic utterances of Scripture concerning both the first and second comings of Jesus Christ. The third Sunday of Advent introduces rejoicing (the traditional *Introit begins, in Lat., *Gaudete*: Phil 4:4). A famous WC series of *antiphons for the season is the *"O" Antiphons. In the EC Advent begins on November 15, forty days before Christmas Day. Colors: purple and/or blue.

Advent wreath. A wreath bearing four *candles, each lit progressively on successive Sundays (or their *eves) of the *Advent season. Its popularity is recent (twentieth century).

affirmation of faith. (1) In the Reformed churches, a formal declaration of belief in Christ given by a person who was either *baptized as an infant within the denomination or baptized outside the denomination. It is the key prerequisite for admitting young people or new congregants to the *Table of the Lord. Its function is thus analogous to *confirmation in the RC (where it is a *sacrament) and the LC. (2) The congregation's *creedal affirmation in the service.

African American spirituals. Christian music rooted in the African American experience, from slavery to the Civil Rights Movement. They particularly emphasize conversion, trusting God through oppression, liberation and home-going. Representative hymns: "Go Tell It on the Mountain," "Going Home," "I Know It Was the Blood," "I've Got Peace Like a River," "Swing Low, Sweet Chariot," "There Is a Balm in Gilead," "Were You There?," "We Shall Overcome," "When the Saints Go Marching In."

agape. Greek *(agapē)* for "love" (cf. 1 Cor 13), liturgically associated with the ancient fellowship meal of early Christians (Jude 12), noted for extending sustenance to the poor (Ign. *Smyrn.* 6.2-7.1). Regular meal gatherings were characteristic of early Christian communities (Pliny, *Epistulae* 10.96; Tert., *Apol.* 39). Early on the *Eucharist may have been associated with it or even referenced by the term (cf. 1 Cor 11:20-22; perhaps *Did.* 9; 10; Ign., *Rom.* 7.3), but later the two meals were separated (cf. the communal meal instructions at *Ap. Trad.* 23.4; 26-30, which includes *prayers, *psalms and a form of *lucernarium*). The Agape likely followed the traditional Greco-Roman meal structure, in other words, first the meal (Gk. *deipnon;* cf. 1 Cor 11:20) followed by drinking (Gk. *symposion;* Lat. *convivium;* cf. Lk 22:20). Christian Roman *cata-comb art would appear to not only blend the two meals (Eucha-rist and Agape), but incorporate the *refrigerium* as well. *See also* Aberkios Inscription; Love Feast.

Agnus Dei. Latin for "Lamb of God," the first two words of a sup-plication based on John 1:29, said or sung in the *Liturgy of the Eucharist and part of the *Ordinary of the Latin *Mass. *See also* Paschal Lamb.

aisle. From Latin *(ala)* for "wing," in historical church architecture running parallel to either side of the *nave, separated from it by a colonnade of pillars. See the appendix.

alb. From Latin *(alba,* f.) for "white," a white priestly *vestment de-rived from the Greco-Roman tunic. Often a simple garment ex-tending to the ankles and belted at the waist, it is usually worn by itself or underneath other official vestments (e.g., *chasubles). The alb is liturgically significant in that it is the Christian *robe of righteousness (*see* baptism) worn by the *ministers during the liturgy on behalf of all baptized believers present in the congre-gation (cf. Rev 3:4; 6:11; 7:9, 13-17; 19:8). A *surplice* is a white outer garment with wide sleeves worn by *priests for certain services as well as by others serving in the worship service.

Alcuin of York (735-804). English monk who oversaw Charle-magne's school at Aachen. The *liberal arts formed the core of the curriculum of the school. Alcuin also modified church liturgy and *lectionary. A thoughtful educator, he contributed greatly to the Carolingian Renaissance and is one of the Irish and Anglo-

Saxon monks who revived learning in western Europe during the early medieval period.

All Saints' Day (November 1). Major observance dating to at least the late fourth century, originally set aside to honor Christian martyrs. Other (non-canonized) deceased Christians are honored the following day, on All the Faithful Departed/All Souls' Day (November 2). Many Protestants, holding that all Christians are saints, honor *all* the Christian departed on All Saints' Day (November 1) or the Sunday following. Historically, the date has varied widely among traditions. The EC celebrates this feast the Sunday following Pentecost, an ancient precedent. *See also* saints, veneration of.

alleluia (hallelujah). Hebrew *(halĕlû yâ)* for "Praise the Lord," an exclamation in many of the *psalms. In Christian liturgy alleluias are responses (cf. *Ap. Trad.* 29C.13-14; Tert., *Or.*, 27). The Alleluia is also a *versicle sung before the *Gospel reading (e.g., Jn 6:68).

altar. A place where *sacrifices are made (Gk. *thusiastērion*; Lat. *altare;* cf. Lat. *altus,* "high"). Sacrifices of various kinds and at various places occur in the OT, but especially in the temple *cult. In historic Christian liturgy, the altar is synonymous with the *Communion *table and the sacrificial death of Jesus (cf. 1 Cor 10:16-20; Ign., *Eph.* 5.2; *Phld.* 4), the table often being coffin-like in shape. Thus in church architecture the *cross is situated above the Communion table; in some traditions the altar is even called "the Cross" or "Golgotha" (Germ. 6; cf. Heb 10:19-21). Irenaeus wrote that the church altar is actually in heaven (*Haer.* 4.18.6; cf. *Sanctus), and indeed Christ in the NT is understood as connecting heaven and earth (Eph 1:10; Col 1:20; cf. Jn 2:19-21).

altar call. In the *revival service of worship, the *invitation to respond positively to the gospel call by coming to the front of the church. The nomenclature of *altar* refers either to the *Communion *rail or the understanding of the new convert sacrificing himself or herself to Christ. The altar call is historically rooted in the frontier "mourners' bench" and Charles Finney's (1792-1875) "anxious seat." *Altar call* can also refer to the traditional gathering of worshipers to pray at the altar that is part of the worship service in the African Methodist Episcopal Church.

ambo. A raised area *(Gk. ambōn)* in a church where the officiating bishop or priest gives the *sermon, analogous to a lectern or *pulpit.

Ambrose, St. (c. 339-397). *Bishop of Milan and advocate of *hymnody within church liturgy. "Savior of the Nations, Come" and "Deus Creator omnium" are attributed to him. He influenced Augustine theologically, also baptizing him (387). A work on the *sacraments is attributed to him (*De sacramentis*).

ambulatory. In church architecture a walking path, usually semicircular, rounding the *altar area (from Lat. *ambulo*, "to walk"). It is perhaps rooted in the ancient act of encircling the powerful dead (cf. Homer, *Iliad* 23.13), pagan counterparts to *saints' relics maintained within the area of the Christian altar (cf. Rev 6:9; see Grabar). See the appendix.

amen. A Hebrew term for "truly" or "so be it," used at the end of a *prayer. In the liturgy it is the important expression of assent by the congregation to the prayers and statements of the *minister.

analogia fidei. A Latin term meaning "analogy of faith" and suggesting that clearer passages of Scripture, and church teaching, should interpret more obscure ones. The *homiletical strategy of finding theological distinctives in all the Scriptures, especially Christian distinctives in the OT, is based on this principle. *See* type, biblical.

Anamnesis. Greek *(anamnēsis)* for "remembrance," the part of the *Eucharistic Prayer in which Christ's suffering, death, resurrection and second coming are proclaimed (cf. 1 Cor 11:26; CCC 1354). The word is found in the institution narratives (Lk 22:19; 1 Cor 11:24-25), and thus the Anamnesis is closely associated with the *Words of Institution (cf. *Ap. Trad.* 4.9-11). Traditionally, anamnesis is not merely a mental act of remembering, but a ritual act of making the past present in some way so that what is taking place in the *Communion service is not merely a retelling but a participation (*koinōnia*) in the *sacrifice of Jesus and his resurrection (CCC 1103, 1362; *see* sacred time).

Anaphora. From the Greek verb *(anapherō)* "to offer up" (e.g., a *sacrifice or *prayer; cf. Heb 7:27; 13:15), a major section of the *Liturgy of the Eucharist. It is evidenced as early as the *Apostolic Tradition* (4.3-13). It incorporates the *Preface, the *Eucharistic Prayer and the *Communion (CCC 1352). The meaning "offering" is indicative that early Christians regarded the Eucharist as an offering to

God given by the congregation (Iren., *Haer.* 4.18.4; CCC 1350).

ancient-future. A paradigmatic approach to liturgical study and implementation that takes into consideration both the history of Christian liturgy in its various stages and the unfolding reality of contemporary thought (Robert Webber, *Ancient-Future: Rethinking Evangelicalism for a Postmodern World,* 1999).

Andrew, Feast of (November 30). The feast in honor of the apostle Andrew Barjonah, a fisherman, brother of the apostle Peter, the first to be called out as a disciple of Jesus (Jn 1:35-40). The feast is associated with the beginning of *Advent, which begins the Sunday nearest November 30. Patron saint of Scotland, Andrew is remembered as the one who first brought someone to meet Jesus (Jn 1:41-42).

Anglican Church. The Church of England, led by the *Archbishop of Canterbury. It was officially founded when Henry VIII separated the Church of England from the RC and the authority of the *bishop of Rome (the pope). Its various forms of worship are found in the *Book of Common Prayer (BCP) and *Common Worship (CW).

Anglican Communion. Those churches that recognize the leadership of the *Archbishop of Canterbury and utilize a version of the *BCP. The latter, however, appears less and less to be a unifying factor.

Annunciation, Feast of the (March 25). A major feast commemorating the angel Gabriel's appearance to the Virgin *Mary (Lk 1:26-38). It is appropriately held nine months before *Christmas Day. The Annunciation is also remembered on the *Ember Wednesday of *Advent, known as the Golden Mass (Lat. *Missa Aurea*). In the early church some considered March 25 the date of the crucifixion. Color: white.

anoint. From Latin (*ungo*) "to smear," as with *oil (and thus also the synonym *unction*). *See* sealing.

anointing of the sick. *See* healing service.

Antecommunion. Literally "before Communion" (Latin *ante,* "before"), the entire part of the service preceding the *Liturgy of the Eucharist. It may become the service itself if the *Eucharist is not celebrated.

anthem. From Latin *antiphona* (and thus at times synonymous with *antiphon), often denoting a musical setting usually sung by a choir and with intensity of expression (e.g., *Handel's *Chandos Anthems*).

antiphon. From Latin *antiphona* (Gk. *antiphōnon*), a brief statement that is sung or said (e.g., after a *psalm or *canticle). It is often composed of material from the *Psalter that is a response of emphasis and also helps to transition to the next *reading. When two choirs (or a *choir and a *cantor) sing alternating verses, they are said to sing *antiphonally*.

Apocrypha. From a Greek term meaning "hidden," a collection of certain Jewish writings contained in the *Septuagint but not found in the Hebrew Bible. As the Septuagint is the version of the OT used by the ancient church, many of these documents are retained in certain Christian Bibles (including originally the *Authorized Version). Though sometimes designated *deuterocanonical* (of a "second canon"), they are often held as authoritative by those churches that retain them. *Readings from these books are assigned within certain liturgies (e.g., the *BCP*).

The RC/WC Apocrypha includes the books of Tobit, Judith, additions to Esther, 1 & 2 Maccabees, Wisdom (of Solomon), Ecclesiasticus (Sirach), Baruch and The Letter of Jeremiah, The Prayer of Azariah and *Song of the Three Jews (both added to the third chapter of Daniel), and Susanna and Bel and the Dragon (both added to Daniel as chapters 13 and 14). The Greek Orthodox Church adds to these 1 Esdras, 3 Maccabees, Psalm 151 (also found at Qumran) and the Prayer of Manasseh. The Russian Orthodox Church also adds 2 Esdras (not part of the Septuagint). Rahlfs's critical edition of the Septuagint also includes 4 Maccabees and the Psalms of Solomon.

Apostles' Creed. An ancient *confession of faith dating to early Christian times, taking on much of its present form by the latter half of the second century. Derived from the *baptismal creed of the church at Rome, it is often a part of WC liturgies. As a baptismal confession, the Creed is appropriately trinitarian, being divided into three parts, each part covering the work of each person of the *Trinity. Orthodox churches, though embracing the *Nicene Creed for liturgical settings, have agreed to the orthodoxy of the Apostles' Creed.

I believe in God, the Father almighty [Gk. *Pantokratōr*],
    maker of heaven and earth;

And in Jesus Christ his only Son our Lord;
    who was conceived by the Holy Spirit,
    born of the Virgin Mary,
    suffered under Pontius Pilate,
    was crucified, dead, and buried.
    He descended into hell.
    The third day he rose again from the dead.
    He ascended into heaven,
    and sits on the right hand of God the Father almighty.
From there he will come to judge the living and the dead.

I believe in the Holy Spirit,
    the holy catholic Church,
    the communion of saints,
    the forgiveness of sins,
    the resurrection of the body,
    and the life everlasting. Amen. (*EBCP,* language updated)

See also Old Roman Creed.

Apostolic Constitutions. A *Syrian collection of rules governing
church liturgy and order (c. late fourth century), influenced by
the *Didache*, the *Apostolic Tradition* and the *Didascalia Apostolorum*. It would itself influence the *Byzantine Rite.

Apostolic Fathers. A category of early Christian literature from
the first and second centuries regarded as within the orthodox
tradition of the Great Church. Works include *1* and *2 Clement*, the
Didache, Ignatius of Antioch's letters, the *Shepherd of Hermas*,
Barnabas, *Diognetus*, the letter of Polycarp and the *Martyrdom of
Polycarp*.

Apostolic Tradition. A historically important early liturgical treatise attributed to Hippolytus (though some question this), parts
of which may reflect Roman liturgy of about the late second century. Originally written in Greek, it has been preserved in other
languages (e.g., Coptic, Ethiopic, Latin, Arabic). Like the *Didache*
and the *Shepherd of Hermas*, this popular text was subject to

expansion(s) over time. Its order for baptism is a witness to an early formulation of the *Apostles' Creed (*see* Old Roman Creed). It also includes an order for the *Liturgy of the Eucharist, as well as many other instructions concerning the church's worship and work. Importantly, it has characteristics in common with the EC. It is titled *Apostolic* because it has long been held within Christendom that the development of liturgy begins with the apostles, if not with Jesus himself (e.g., the *Lord's Prayer).

apse. From Latin for "arch" (*apsis;* Gk. *konchē,* "shell"), the semicircular area at the *altar end of a church, rooted in the *basilica form. Sometimes associated with its vault is a representation of the *dome of heaven. This "shell" feature has also been associated with both Jesus' birth and death (Germ. 3), and thus it is appropriate that baptismal *fonts have been associated with apses. See the appendix.

archbishop. The chief *bishop, perhaps presiding over a significant geographical area or a specific group of believers united by theology and/or *rite.

Archbishop of Canterbury. The reigning *bishop over the Church of England and the *Anglican Communion and whose seat is at *Canterbury.

art, Christian. *See* catacombs, Christian Roman; Jesus (iconography).

Articles of Religion (1553, 1571). The statement of faith of the *Anglican Church, often referred to as The Thirty-nine Articles, and printed in the *BCP.* Theologically it is informed to some extent by both Lutheran and *Reformed theologies.

Ascension Day. A major feast celebrated on the fortieth day from *Easter and commemorating the ascension of Jesus to heaven forty days after his resurrection (Acts 1:3, 9). As it always falls on a Thursday, it is often commemorated on the Sunday following (Ascension Sunday). Color: white.

asceticism. Derived from the Greek term "to labor, to exercise" (*askeō*), the denial of normal physical needs and pleasures. It is rooted in Greek philosophy (e.g., the Pythagoreans). In Plato's *Phaedo* Socrates teaches that the true philosopher practices dying (80e-81a, 82c), in other words, puts off satisfying the desires of the body, since the soul is the true person and longs to be free of the body. Christians, to various degrees, have embraced ascetic practices for spiritual ends (*see* abstinence; virgin).

Ash Wednesday. A major fast (WC) on the first day of *Lent. Preceded in some cultures by a period of revelry (e.g., carnival), it is a day of repentance that begins the Lenten season of somber reflection on Christ's approaching *Passion. Ashes are placed on the forehead as an act of repentance (cf. Job 42:6; Is 58:5; Jon 3:5-6). Color: purple or uncolored linen.

Athanasian Creed. An important *confession of faith concerning the *Trinity and Christology, popular in the WC. Dating to the fifth or early sixth centuries, and also known as the *Quicunque Vult*, it is traditionally recited on *Trinity Sunday.

Authorized Version. The English translation of the Bible commissioned by King James I of England and published in 1611. Colloquially it is known as the King James Version. It originally included the *Apocrypha.

Ave Maria. Latin meaning "Hail, Mary," a *prayer to the Virgin *Mary, with elements taken from the blessings declared for her by the angel Gabriel and by her kinswoman Elizabeth in the Gospel of Luke (Lk 1:28, 42). The text is comprised of two parts, the first established in the eleventh century and historically coinciding with the rise of the medieval *cult of the Virgin, the second in the sixteenth century:

Hail Mary, full of grace,
the Lord is with thee.
Blessed art thou among women,
and blessed is the fruit of thy womb, Jesus.

Holy Mary, Mother of God,
pray for us sinners, now,
and in the hour of our death.
Amen.

Recited in the RC (though no longer part of the *Office) and by some *Anglicans, the prayer has been set to music, most famously the music of Franz Schubert and *Bach.

B

baby dedication. A *rite of initiation for newborns/infants and their parents, usually performed by the *minister during corporate worship. It is often practiced by those churches that do not perform infant baptism (*see* baptism, infant), with emphasis on the parents' commitment to raise the child in Christian nurture.

Bach, Johann Sebastian (1685-1750). A German Lutheran composer of the Baroque period of Western music who is considered one of the greatest composers of church music. Both an innovator and standardizer, he wrote music in a number of forms. About two hundred of his church *cantatas are extant. His *Passions are considered the greatest. Also notable among his religious works is the Mass in B minor with its moving choruses, a work that makes free use of the traditional *Mass form. Four of his sons went on to musical careers, one tutoring Mozart, another influencing Haydn. Representative hymns and settings: "Sleepers, Awake" (from Cantata No. 140, *Wachet auf*); "O Sacred Head Now Wounded"; "A Mighty Fortress Is Our God" (from Cantata No. 80).

baldachino. A canopy over a throne, altar or tomb, which is a version of the *dome of heaven. Such a structure stood over the Ark of the Covenant (Ex 30:6; Josephus, *Jewish Antiquities* 8.103) and can be found over some church *altars, which are themselves sometimes equated with the Ark (cf. Germ. 4 and 5: *"ciborium"). The most famous is that over the high altar of *St. Peter's, Rome, designed by Bernini (1624-1633).

banner. An artistically decorated length of cloth displayed in the worship service, its color often corresponding to the liturgical season or celebration.

baptism. From Greek "to immerse" (*baptizō*), the Christian *rite of initiation into the *church (Acts 2:38, 41; 9:18; 19:4-5). The ritual involves the element of *water, with the initiate sprinkled, poured on or immersed. Baptism in the name of the *Trinity is integral to the Great Commission (Mt 28:18-20) and is thus the visible evidence of the advancement of the gospel of Jesus Christ in the world.

Theologically, one is baptized *into Christ* (Rom 6:3; Gal 3:27) and thereafter is *in Christ* (Gal 3:28; 2 Cor 5:17). To be baptized is to be identified with, or to participate in, Christ's death, burial and resurrection (Rom 6:1-11, esp. 3-5), in other words, to die and rise with Christ (Col 2:12-13; cf. Eph 2:5-6; Gal 2:20; 2 Tim 2:11). It is a ritual rebirth (Tit 3:5; Jn 3:3-5; 1 Pet 1:3, 23; Cyr., *Myst. Cat.* 2.4; cf. *Gospel of Thomas* 4) brought about by the Holy Spirit (Jn 3:6), the gift of whom is connected with baptism (Acts 2:38; 19:5-6).

Baptism is also associated with forgiveness of sins (Mk 1:4; Acts 2:38; *Barn.* 6.11; Justin, *1 Apol.* 61), the rite described as a *washing* (Gk. *loutron*: Eph 5:26; Tit 3:5; Cyr., *Procatech.* 2, 7). The Christian, as a result of baptism, is clothed/robed with Christ (Gal 3:27; cf. Col 3:10; Mk 16:5; Herm., *Sim.* 9.16.2, 3), the conscience "clean" (Heb 10:22). The person who emerges after baptism is a *new creation* (2 Cor 5:17; cf. Gal 3:27-28; Rev 21:1-3; *Barn.* 16.8). The Christian in this life participates to some extent in the resurrection life (Rom 6:11; Col 2:13; 3:1; Eph 2:5-6), in other words, in "newness of life" (Rom 6:4).

Early baptismal rites are preserved by Justin Martyr (*1 Apol.* 61), the *Apostolic Tradition* (20-21) and Cyril of Jerusalem. Historically, baptism is preceded by a period of instruction (*see* catechumenate). In the *Apostolic Tradition*, after three years of instruction and as the day of the ritual drew near, baptism was soberly anticipated with *exorcisms (20.3, 8), *ablutions (20.5), *prayer and *fasting (20.7; cf. *Did.* 7.4; Paul at Acts 9:8-19), and finally a Saturday night vigil of further instruction by the *bishop (20.9) followed by baptism early Sunday morning (21.1), perhaps the morning of *Easter.

In ancient baptism the initiate renounced the devil and evil while facing *west (Cyr., *Myst. Cat.* 1.2, 4), and then confessed the faith (*Ap. Trad.* 21.12-18; cf. Eph 4:5) while facing *east (Cyr., *Myst. Cat.* 1.9). The initiate was baptized nude (*Ap. Trad.* 21.3; Cyr., *Myst. Cat.* 2.2; cf. Col 3:9-11; *Gospel of Thomas* 37; *catacombs and *sarcophagi art; see Scroggs and Groff), symbolizing a return to the pre-Fall Adamic state or the new Adam (Eph 4:22-24; cf. 1 Cor 15:47-49). Additionally, baptism involved *sealing with *oil (symbol of the Holy Spirit), receiving new clothes (Cyr., *Myst. Cat.* 1.10), being joyously welcomed into the congregation and participating that day in first *Communion. Some of these elements of ancient baptism are retained among various Christian churches to this day. Traditionally the most popular days for the occasion of baptism are *Easter, *Pentecost and *Epiphany, each having baptismal significance (cf. Tert., *Bapt.* 19). OT types for baptism include Noah and the ark (1 Pet 3:20-21) and the crossing of the Red Sea (1 Cor 10:1-2).

In the classical Protestant tradition baptism is held to be one of two *sacraments of the church, understood as a sign and a seal/promise of one's salvation in Christ. It is also held as a sign of the redemptive covenant between God and his people, and thus is extended to *infants as circumcision was to the male Hebrew children (cf. Col 2:11-12; Heid. Cat. 69-73; West. Conf. 28; Aug. Conf. 9). Other Protestants view baptism as an *ordinance, the Christian's obedient demonstration of commitment to Christ (e.g., BF&M 7). Color: white or red.

baptism, believers'. The view, rooted in the RR, that baptism is only for those able to profess faith in Christ (i.e., older children and adults). A consequence of this view is that those baptized as infants are to be "rebaptized" (from which was derived the name *Anabaptists*, from Greek, "to baptize again"). The position is based on (1) the fact that there is no clear directive in Scripture to baptize the very young, and (2) there is no clear evidence of baptism for infants before the second half of the second century (for historical discussion see Wright). *See also* baptism, infant.

Baptism, Eucharist and Ministry **(1982).** An important and influential ecumenical document issued by the World Council of Churches to enhance Christian *unity and witness.

baptism in the Holy Spirit. In Pentecostal theology, the post-conversion special reception of, and empowerment by, the Holy Spirit. The empowerment is evidenced by the experience of the *charismata*, in particular speaking in tongues (Acts 2:1-4; 10:44-46). Other important texts include Mark 1:8; Acts 1:4-5, 8; 2:1-4; 11:15-16. This *Spirit* baptism is not to be confused with water *baptism.

baptism, infant. The application of the *rite of *baptism to infants and small children. Scriptural support for this position is of two kinds. First, baptism of small children is analogous to Jewish circumcision (Col 2:11-12), both rites being entrances into their respective religions. Second, Jesus commanded the little children to be brought to him (Mk 10:14, a chapter with baptismal referents). Third, the whole household of the Philippian jailor was baptized upon *his* conversion (Acts 16:31-33). The rite is quite ancient, the *Apostolic Tradition* mentioning those unable to speak for themselves at baptism (21.4). As part of the rite, the parents and congregation are assured of God's promise to the child (Acts 2:39) and they respond with the promise to raise and train the child in the ways of the Lord. Infant baptism is practiced by the AC, LC, P&RC, RC and Methodist churches. Such churches often have a later rite of *confirmation or profession of faith. Confessional statements: Aug. Conf. 9; Heid. Cat. 74; West. Conf. 28.4; CCC 1250-52; cf. Calvin, *Institutes* 4.16.

Baptism of Our Lord. A feast day that commemorates Jesus' *baptism in the Jordan River by *John the Baptist. It now tends to be celebrated the *Sunday following the celebration of *Epiphany since the meanings of the two feasts are related.

baptismal promises, renewal of. A *rite that reaffirms the promises guaranteed the believer when originally *baptized, as well as the confession of faith the believer made at baptism. Though sometimes called *renewal of baptismal vows*, most understand baptism as God's gift, not a contract (*vow* from Lat. *votum*, implying *do ut des*), though Paul encouraged Christians to reflect on their own baptisms in relation to manner of life (Rom 6:1-8; Gal 5:24-25). Opportune times to renew the promises include *Lent, *Easter or any time the rite of baptism is performed during the year. Corporate recitation of the *Apostles' Creed also hearkens back to baptism.

baptistery. A place set aside for the *baptismal rite. In earlier times (into the Middle Ages) the baptistery was often a separate building (or separate room as at *Dura-Europos). Today baptisteries (or just *fonts) are usually incorporated into the church interior, though some may opt for a more natural setting (river, coastal shore) or the intimate setting of a residential pool. Architecturally, early baptisteries were usually based on funerary architecture (see Grabar; cf. Rom 6:3-4), incorporating *domes or *baldachinos, and sometimes *ambulatories. Frequently they were round or *octagonal.

basilica. From Latin for "royal," the earliest widespread plan of freestanding *church buildings, based on a Roman civil architectural form. Still influential today, its basic components include the *nave, *aisles, *apse, and sometimes the *ambulatory and *transept. A number of the earliest Roman Christian basilicas were not actually "churches" but were associated with tombs, in which case they were either *coemeteria subteglata* (basically indoor cemeteries) intended for communal funerary banqueting (e.g., S. Agnese and SS. Marcellino e Pietro in Rome; *see refrigerium*) or *martyria* (memorial funerary buildings over a martyr's grave), known as *basilicae ad corpus*. *Old St. Peter's (in Rome) merged the two categories (see Krautheimer). See the appendix.

Baumstark, Anton (1872-1948). The scholar whose groundbreaking *Comparative Liturgy* (originally Fr. 1940; Eng. translation of Fr. third ed. 1958) became a benchmark for modern liturgical scholarship, advocating a comparative method for the historical study of "liturgical evolution."

Bede, "Venerable" (c. 672-735). The learned Anglo-Saxon Benedictine *monk and historian. Raised first at St. Peter at Wearmouth *monastery in northern England, then at the nearby *St. Paul's at Jarrow, where he remained for the rest of his life. His most famous work is *History of the English Church and People* (731, written in Latin). Like *Alcuin of York, Bede was a Western Dark Age scholar and was a supporter of the Roman church's liturgy (especially the *Daily Office) as well as a proponent of the *liberal arts in education. He is now buried in Durham *Cathedral.

bell. An instrument to call people to attention or *prayer (*see also* chimes) and to emphasize momentous occasions. Used at the *Sanctus and the Elevation of the *Host (RC).

bema. From a Greek word meaning "step," the raised *chancel area (the *sanctuary) in EC architecture, separated from the congregation by the *iconostasis.

Benedicamus (Domino). Latin for "Let us bless (the Lord)," said by the *minister, with the congregation responding, "Thanks be to God."

Benedicite, Omnia Opera Domini. *See* Song of the Three Jews.

Benedict, St. (480-547). The *monk who standardized *monastery life in the WC. The activities (*prayer, study and work) and *vows of monastic life were given in his *Rule*.

benediction. From Latin "to bless" (*benedico*), the blessing of God's care given by the *minister at the end of the service. Aaron's Blessing is traditional (Num 6:24-26, introduced into the liturgy by *Luther; cf. Ps 4:6; 67:1), as is Paul's to the Corinthians: "The grace of the Lord Jesus Christ, the love of God, and the communion of the Holy Spirit be with all of you" (2 Cor 13:13; note also 1 Thess 5:23; Jude 24-25).

Benedictus (Dominus Deus). *See* Song of Zechariah.

Benedictus Es, Domine. *See* Song of the Three Jews.

Benedictus Qui Venit. Latin for "Blessed is the one who comes," the triumphant proclamation of the crowd on *Palm Sunday as Jesus rode into Jerusalem (Mt 21:9; Ps 118:26). The exclamation in Christian liturgy follows the *Sanctus, and contains the cry "Hosanna!"

Bible. The *Word of God, and thus foundational to and inseparable from Christian corporate worship (1 Tim 4:13; 2 Tim 4:2). The Bible is the primary *liturgical book, containing *prayers, *hymns and *rites, as well as sacred stories, much of it originally intended for use in corporate worship.

bishop. From Greek for "overseer" (Gk. *episkopos*), an ordained church officer overseeing a particular area called a *diocese*. The qualifications of the office are given at 1 Timothy 3:1-7. In the ancient church the office of bishop became an exalted position, the letters of Ignatius of Antioch (c. 110) revealing an elevated description of the bishop (e.g., Ign., *Magn.* 6.1). The church at Rome did not clearly evidence a monarchical bishop until about the latter half of the second century (Ignatius in his letter to the Roman church addresses no bishop), though even by the early second century Roman church officials had strengthened their authority by analogies with officiants of the OT sacrificial *cult (*1 Clem.* 40-44). The bishop's seat in a church became known as his "throne" (*see* cathedral), perhaps a lingering aspect of the divine status of the ruler in the ancient Near East.

blended worship. *See* convergence service.

blessing. An *invocation or expression of God's favor, as at the beginning of the service when the minister says, "The Lord be with you" (cf. Boaz's blessing at Ruth 2:4; Jn 20:19). *Blessing* is also an expression of *consecration, as well as *praise (Ps 34:1: "I will bless the Lord at all times; / his praise shall continually be in my mouth").

Blue Christmas. A liturgical service of recent innovation that provides a pre-Christmas service of reflection for those for whom

*Christmas, for whatever reason, is not a happy time. Since the service takes place around December 21, it is also known as Longest Night (*see* solstice).

Book of Common Prayer (BCP). The *liturgical service book of the Church of England. Those churches in communion with the Church of England (AC) have their own versions. The first two editions were produced during the reign of *Edward VI by *Cranmer (1549, 1552). The 1662 revision is the current version in the *Anglican Church. Comprehensive and of high literary character, the Anglican *Book of Common Prayer (ABCP)* has been esteemed for centuries, even by non-Anglicans. It includes orders for the *Daily Office, the *Eucharist, *baptism, *burial, *ordination, *marriage and other *occasional offices, the *Sunday and Daily Office *lectionaries, a great many *canticles, *collects, *prayers and the *Great Litany, Coverdale's translation (rev.) of the *Psalter, *Articles of Religion, and *catechism. John Wesley developed a modified edition for North American Methodists (1784). The American Episcopal *Book of Common Prayer (EBCP)* (1789) was partly influenced by the Scottish *BCP* (1637); the latest edition of the *EBCP* is that of 1979.

In the Anglican Church the *BCP* is now supplemented with a series of books titled *Common Worship*, which offers a variety of alternative forms for worship and is the culmination of a number of revision attempts. Indeed, while the *ABCP* revision of 1928 was rejected by Parliament (*The 1928 Prayer Book*), many of the orders found their way into the later *Alternative Service Book of 1980 [ASB]*, as well as *A Lectionary and Additional Collects for Holy Communion* (2001) and the aforementioned *Common Worship* (which replaced the *ASB* in 2000). Among other branches of the AC, alternative or supplemental service books have been developed (e.g., Canada, 1985, and Australia, 1995).

Book of Hours. A medieval book, sometimes colorfully illustrated, containing devotional *offices (e.g., for the Virgin *Mary and the dead), *prayers and *psalms. The most famous illustrators of Books of Hours were the Limbourg brothers (fl. turn of the fifteenth century). The books, written in Latin or the vernacular, were usually for individual use by *lay people. The illustrations today offer a window into the lives of medieval people. *See also* cult of the Virgin; Office for the Dead.

Book of Kells. Named after an *abbey in Ireland, the most famous of early medieval illuminated manuscripts (c. 800). Containing the Gospels in Latin, it exemplifies the "insular" artistic style. Like some other illuminated manuscripts of the time, for example, the Lindisfarne Gospels (c. 700), it was produced in a *monastery that served as a Western Dark Age outpost of learning.

Bradbury, William B. (1816-1868). An American composer of *hymn tunes. Among his most familiar musical settings are those for "Jesus Loves Me," "Just As I Am," "Sweet Hour of Prayer" and "The Solid Rock."

bread. A basic food of sustenance that figures prominently in ancient Jewish and Christian religion. The OT tabernacle/temple showbread (Ex 25:30; 2 Chron 2:4; Heb 9:2) was always on display in the sacred precinct, indicative of God's constant provision, as was the manna in the wilderness (Ex 16, esp. v. 15; Jn 6:49-51; *Ap. Trad.* 21.31; cf. Rev 2:17). Bread is also one of the two elements of the central *rite of Christian worship, the *Eucharist, in which Jesus Christ continuously feeds his people. *See also* Lord's Prayer, the.

Breaking of the Bread. The ceremonial breaking (fraction) of the *consecrated *bread following the *Eucharistic Prayer. It is indicative of Jesus as the *sacrifice for sins (1 Cor 11:24). In this breaking of bread Jesus is known (Lk 24:30-31; cf. Jn 21:12-14), and the Christian community enjoys the reality of Christian *unity (Acts 2:42).

breviary. From Latin for "abridgment" *(breviarium),* a *liturgical book containing prescribed *readings, *prayers, inspirational *lessons, etc., for the *Daily Office.

burial rites. *See* funerary rites.

Byzantine religious art. The ecclesiastical artistic style that, while retaining such classical distinctives as order and restraint, is characterized by idealism (rather than realism), *symbolism and other-world vision. *See also* icon.

Byzantine Rite. The *Rite of the *Greco-Russian Orthodox tradition, developed at Constantinople during the eastern Roman Empire. Incorporating elements of earlier liturgies (e.g., those of Chrysostom and Basil), the earliest extant witness to the Byzantine Rite is the codex known as Barberini *gr.* 336 (c. 800).

C

Caedmon's Hymn. An ancient Old English *hymn composed by the Anglo-Saxon *priest Caedmon (seventh century).

calendar, Christian. Calendar followed by Christians for marking various religious observances. It is primarily composed of two parts: (1) *Sunday worship and (2) the *liturgical year. Depending on the tradition, the calendar may also include the *sanctoral cycle.

call to worship. The opening words of the worship service spoken by the *minister or sung by the *choir.

Calvin, John (1509-1564). A second-generation reformer whose theological views came to dominate first *Geneva and then generally the P&RC. His liturgical distinctives include the *prayer for illumination before the *readings, weekly *Eucharist (often ignored by his followers, both contemporary and modern), heavenly *union with Christ at the Eucharist and the metrical *Genevan *Psalter. His liturgical *La Forme des prières et chantz ecclésiatiques* (Eng. *Form of Prayers*) was published in 1542.

campanile. Italian term for a free-standing bell tower associated with a church (e.g., the Leaning Tower of Pisa).

candle. A human implement for dispelling darkness. Important element of Christian worship symbolizing (1) Christ as the light of the world (Lat. *Lux mundi*), (2) the light of God's *Word and, in general, (3) the presence of God. Ceremonial candles are often presented to the newly *baptized and *confirmed, and lighted candles may also pay tribute to the ongoing life of the deceased in Christ. *See also* Paschal candle.

Candlemas (February 2). A major feast, also known as The Presentation of Christ in the Temple or The Purification of Mary (Lk 2:22-39; cf. Lev 12:1-4). Celebrated the fortieth day from *Christmas Day, it is the absolute end of the *Christmas season in the Christian year. The *Nunc Dimittis is especially associated with this day, as it originates in Luke's narrative. In Jerusalem the celebration dates to the mid-fourth century where it originally was celebrated on February 14, giving a date of January 6 for Jesus' nativity (= 40 days). Color: white.

canon. Standard, or rule (Gk. *kanōn*, "measuring rod"), as in the "canon of Scripture," those books comprising the *Word of God, and "Canon of the Mass," the authoritative form of the *Eucharistic Prayer in the RC. A *canon* is also a member of the *clergy frequently associated with a *cathedral.

Canon of the Eucharist. *See* Eucharistic Prayer.

Canon of the Mass. *See* Eucharistic Prayer.

Canonical Hours. *See* Daily Office.

cantata. An Italian term meaning "sung," a musical term of various meanings. However, in light of *Bach's well-known cantatas, in the context of worship it is used of multipassage musical settings of biblical texts involving voices and instruments. These *cantatas* are somewhat similar to *oratorios, though much shorter in length.

Cantemus Domino. *See* Song of Moses.

Canterbury Cathedral. An early Norman and Gothic *cathedral located in Canterbury, England, and dedicated in 1130. It is the official seat of the *Archbishop of Canterbury.

canticle. From Latin for "a little song" (*canticulum*), a religious song. Many canticles used in liturgies are taken from the Scriptures. The *EBCP* uses the following non-Psalter canticles ([B] = *Byzantine Rite as well; for those without asterisk *see* Songs of Isaiah):

*Benedicite, Omnia Opera Domini [B]	The *Song of Moses [B]
*Benedictus Es, Domine [B]	Ecce, Deus
*Magnificat [B]	Quaerite Dominum
*Benedictus Dominus Deus [B]	Surge, Illuminare
*Nunc Dimittis	*Kyrie Pantocrator
*Gloria in Excelsis Deo	*Dignus Es
*Te Deum	*Magna et Mirabilia

Other canticles recited in much of the Byzantine Rite are

Prayer of Hannah (1 Sam 2:1-10)
Prayer of Habakkuk (Hab 3:2-19)
Prayer of Isaiah (Is 26:9-20)
Prayer of Jonah (Jon 2:2[3]-9[10])

Canticles. Another name for the Song of Solomon in the OT. The text likely reflects, in part, ancient Near Eastern liturgical influences. In Jewish tradition it is read at *Passover.

cantor. A soloist who *chants/sings various parts of the liturgy.

cantus firmus. Latin for "fixed song," a fixed melody, perhaps traditional, undergirding a layer(s) of melodious innovation.

capitulum. Latin for "chapter," a short Scripture *reading in the
*Daily Office. The "Capitular Office," which includes a martyrol-
ogy reading, historically followed immediately by the *office of
Prime.

carol. Songs sung *strophically.

Carrington, Philip (1892-1975). Anglican *archbishop of Quebec
who proposed in his *The Primitive Christian Calendar* (1952) that
the Gospel of Mark is a liturgical text. Carrington argued that the
lecture divisions in the *Codex Vaticanus version of Mark, for the
most part, were intrinsic to the finished compositional nature of
the work and reflected an ancient Christian year/calendar. He was
also instrumental in the development of the Canadian *BCP* (1962).

cassock. A long ecclesiastical garment, sometimes worn under a
surplice. *See also* alb; robe.

catacombs, Christian Roman. From the Latin *ad Catacumbas* ("near
the hollow"), the traditional name for the funerary area beneath
Basilica S. Sebastiano, now applied to all the ancient underground
cemeteries found outside the periphery of ancient Rome. The
catacombs were, generally speaking, neither places of refuge nor
frequent corporate worship (but *see* basilica), though they were
visited by the ancient Roman church (Jerome, *Comm. Ezech.* 12.40).
They mainly consist of many miles of corridors (*galleries*) with
loculi (burial slots carved into the gallery walls). Those who could
afford larger burial presences might be buried in *cubicula* (rooms
attached to the galleries, accommodating a number of burials).
The earliest burials and associated art date from about the turn
of the third century.

The catacombs are the source for most extant early Christian art,
especially pre-Constantinian. Significant *symbols include the *fish,
*dove and anchor, and expressions of "in peace" (Gk. *EN EIRHNH*;
Lat. *IN PACE*; see Snyder) are common. Catacomb paintings tend
to be found in and near the wealthier *cubicula*. Frequent painted
representations include the *Good Shepherd, *Jonah and the sea
creature, the raising of *Lazarus, the healing of the paralytic, the
*orans, Noah and the ark, and banquets (*see refrigerium*). There are

no representations of the crucifixion, though a cross is to be found in the ceiling pattern of many *cubicula* (*see* dome of heaven).

Early on the Roman church looked upon the care of the cemetery as a ministry (*Ap. Trad.* 40; Hippolytus, *Refutation of All Heresies* 9.7), and thus the stunning miles of stacked *loculi* are evidence of Christian **koinōnia* and *agapē*. One of the earliest catacomb cemeteries is named after Flavia Domitilla, wife of Titus Flavius Clemens of the Flavian *gens*, both likely Christians (Suetonius, *Domitianus* 15.1), who perhaps bequeathed the property to the church. Early bishops of Rome are buried in the S. Callisto catacomb, in the Crypt of the Popes, which dates from the third century.

catechism. From Greek *(katēcheō)* "to instruct" (cf. Lk 1:4; Acts 18:25), a document often structured in a question-and-answer format that teaches basic doctrine. Among the more famous are Luther's Small Catechism (1529; Lutheran), the Heidelberg Catechism (1563; Reformed), the Westminster Shorter and Larger Catechisms (1647, 1648; Presbyterian), and the *Catechism of the Catholic Church* (1994; RC). Some churches teach their catechisms within a simplified worship service (e.g., some LC and Reformed churches).

catechumenate. A system for preparing individuals for *baptism over a period of time. Early directives include the **Apostolic Tradition* (17-19), and the earliest extant record of teaching is that of *Bishop Cyril of Jerusalem (mid-fourth century), which took place at the *Church of the Holy Sepulchre. Post-baptismal instruction following Easter is known as *mystagogy, the explanation of the initiatory rites of baptism and *Eucharist. The decline of the catechumenate in antiquity was due to the increase of infant baptism (*see* baptism, infant).

cathedral. *Church building containing the seat (Gk. *kathedra*) of a *bishop.

celebrant. One who leads the congregation in the *Liturgy of the Eucharist.

cena pura. Latin, meaning "pure supper," adopted from Jewish nomenclature for the Friday evening meal (the *eve of the Sabbath) that perhaps included *fish, and applied to Christian *Communion (see Horbury), especially on *Good Friday (Rome, fourth century).

censer. A container of burning *incense, usually with a chain attached; also called a *thurible*.

ceremony. A formal act or event, one that follows a particular *form.

chalice. A cup or goblet holding the *eucharistic *wine (Lat. *calix*; Gk. *kylix*).

chancel. The area around and inclusive of the *altar/*Communion *table in a WC that in former times was marked off from the rest of the church interior by a lattice screen (Lat. *cancellus*), and may still be marked off by the altar *rail. It corresponds to the EC *sanctuary. *See also* bema.

chant. From Latin *cantus*, "song," the non-metered singing of set liturgical texts. It is retained to a variable degree in the high liturgical churches. By chanting or singing the *whole* liturgy, the EC retains the ancient custom of singing *cult-related texts (e.g., Homer, the *Homeric Hymns*, Pindar and Greek tragedy, as well as the Jewish *Psalter, even the Jewish *Passover Seder today), a conviction that declined in the West. *See also* Mass, plainsong.

chapel. From Latin *cappella*, a small church or room designed for worship, either independent of or attached to a larger *church building.

charismata. From Greek *charisma*, "gift," the gifts of the Holy Spirit manifested in corporate worship (1 Cor 12, 14). *Pentecostal and charismatic worship services are marked by openness to *spontaneity and therefore, in some services, the more spectacular gifts (e.g., tongues and healing), manifestations of Spirit-led diversity within Christian *unity. Some charismatic churches relegate the expression of certain gifts to a less public gathering.

Chartres Cathedral. A High *Gothic *cathedral in Chartres, France, dedicated (1260) to the Virgin *Mary.

chasuble. A priestly outer garment, especially worn at the *Eucharist in some WC. *See also* cope.

Cherubic Hymn. The great *hymn (*Cheroubikon*) sung near the beginning of the *eucharistic rite in the EC, the moment corresponding to the *offertory in the WC.

Chi Rho. An ancient symbol of Christ involving the first two Greek letters of *Christos*, often flanked by the Greek letters Α and Ω (Rev 1:8) and sometimes forming a *cross. Called the monogram, or *labarum*, it is perhaps the sign that Constantine saw at the Milvian Bridge (Lactantius, *The Deaths of the Persecutors* 44; Eusebius, *Life of Constantine* 1.28, 31).

children's sermon. A short lesson for children in the congregation before the *Liturgy of the Word, often given by someone other than the presiding *minister. The subject matter may coincide with either the liturgical day or the theme of the main *sermon. Children are usually invited forward to the front of the church to hear the sermon and afterwards dismissed to rejoin their families in the pews or exit to some other program designed for them. The children's sermon affirms the importance of children as part of the church family and functions as a way for children to adapt to the main service.

chimes. A variation of *bells generated by an *organ, often used to call the congregants to attention as the service is about to begin.

choir. Also spelled *quire*: (1) a group of appointed singers for the liturgy (e.g., David's singers at 1 Chron 25; cf. Ezra 3:11); (2) the section of the church interior where the clergy are seated, part of the *altar end of the interior (*see* chancel; sanctuary). It is called the *choir* because often the singers were situated in this area of the *church building (in the Middle Ages liturgical singing was done only by the *ministers, *cantor and choir). Some churches today place the choir (1) in the rear balcony of the church building.

chorale. A *hymn tune for corporate singing (especially in the German LC). Also another name for a choir.

chrism. An ancient Christian ritual of *anointing with *oil (from Gk. *chrisma*, "anointing oil"). It is usually connected with *baptism and the *sealing with the Holy Spirit. In this respect chrism parallels the descent of the Holy Spirit at Jesus' baptism (Mk 1:10). Some early Christian groups tended to emphasize chrism as a separate *rite or *sacrament.

chrismation. An EC *rite corresponding to WC *confirmation. *See* sealing.

Christ the King, Feast of. Established in 1925 by Pope Pius XI and celebrated on the final Sunday of the WC calendar (falling between November 20 and 26). Color: white.

Christmas carol. A musical piece sung in celebration of *Christmas. Though carols *per se* are songs sung *strophically, the term *Christmas carol* has come to include a wide variety of music traditionally sung around Christmastime, including *hymns and *chants, and extends to music originally not specifically intended for the Feast of Christmas, including music from *Advent, *New Year's, *Epiphany, *Candlemas and even the *Annunciation. For example, *"O Come, O Come, Emmanuel" is an Advent *antiphon, "Good King Wenceslas" celebrates the Feast of St. *Stephen (Boxing Day), "Coventry Carol" recalls the Holy *Innocents, "Deck the Halls" is a New Year's song, and "We Three Kings" belongs to Epiphany (see Keyte and Parrott).

Christmas Day (December 25). A major feast celebrating the birth of Christ. In earlier times the EC celebrated Christmas on January 6 (the Armenian Church retains this later date). The commemoration dates to at least 336 (Rome). The date was also significant in antiquity as the birthday of Mithras. Astronomically the date is closely associated with the winter *solstice, the shortest day of the year. Thereafter, for the next six months, the length of daylight *increases* with every passing day, and thus December 25 is associated with the birth of a new year, or *New Year's Day, and was well known as the date for the birth of the sun in ancient Rome (*Natalis Solis Invicti*). Metaphorically, such a date could be connected with the birth of a significant person, as for example, a new cycle of time is associated with the birth of an Apollo-like hero in the *Fourth Eclogue* of Virgil (c. 37 B.C.). While there are disputes about whether Christianity took the date over from Mithras or Mithraism from Christianity, the impulse to celebrate Christ's birth on December 25 is likely more deeply rooted in the culture of the Hellenistic world. Indeed, a well-known iconographic theme of the ancient church is Jesus as Helios (the sun = *Sol Invictus*; cf. Mal 4:2) on the chariot pulled by horses (the *quadriga*), a fine example being that in the Tomb of the Julii of the necropolis beneath *St. Peter's at Rome. With Jesus all of creation enjoys its rebirth, or new creation (cf. Rev 1:12-18, where Jesus is presented in the imagery of a triumphant Helios). Thus December 25 is not only appropriate to celebrate the newborn infant Jesus in his first advent, but the triumphant Jesus of the second coming brings to a close the further prophetic anticipation of the *Advent season. Color: white.

The date of December 25 may have also at one time commemorated the Cana wedding event (Jn 2:1-12), a *pericope evoking Dionysian imagery of miraculous wine production at a wedding, with concepts of fertility and new life/beginnings apparent. The *Annunciation is celebrated nine months before Christmas Day.

Christmas (Feast of Our Lord's Nativity). A festival commemorating the birth of Jesus Christ, with emphasis on the incarnation (*Immanuel*, "God with us"). It begins on December 25 and traditionally ends late January 5 (the eve of *Epiphany, or Twelfth Night), thus making twelve days for the entire festival of Christmas, though now some conclude the Christmas season the Sunday following Epiphany Sunday. Color: white.

Chrysostom, Divine Liturgy of. The liturgy attributed to St. John Chrysostom (c. 349-407), *bishop of Constantinople (previously a priest at Antioch), and later designated one of the Doctors of the Church. It is the basis of many liturgies in the EC (e.g., the *Byzantine Rite).

Chrysostom, Prayer of. A prayer from the Liturgy of *Chrysostom used in the *EBCP* as a closing prayer in the *Daily Office.

church. A collective term for Christians (Gk. *kyriakon*, from *kyriakos*, "the Lord's own"; also Gk. *ekklēsia*; Lat. *ecclesia*, from which Spanish *iglesia*), the body of Christ, the community of *baptized believers.

church building. The physical locale of Christian worship and center of Christian communal life. As was the case with most Eastern *cults in the Roman period, and even Jewish synagogues, Christian congregations often met in homes (Acts 2:46; Rom 16:5; 1 Cor 16:19) that formed around family households (1 Cor 1:16; 16:15) and thus defined the original "church" (cf. CCC 2685; *see also* Dura-Europos, church building of). Later stand-alone churches often followed the *basilica form in architecture, with WC buildings generally taking a Latin *cruciform plan, EC buildings often a centralized cruciform plan, and with both plans nearly always orientated toward the *east. (In the EC the centralized church building symbolizes the church as a womb.) Medieval *Romanesque and *Gothic cathedrals were built on the Western basilica form, and the medieval interior plan was revisited in many nineteenth-

and twentieth-century British and American churches.

As a result of the Protestant Reformation, the importance of the *sermon began to dictate church architecture in the P&RC, with the *pulpit becoming more elevated and lengthy naves yielding to new layouts that would meet auditory needs (*see* Hingham Meetinghouse; Wren, Sir Christopher). With the popularity of the *revival service of worship and the *contemporary worship service, modern evangelical churches have tended toward auditorium-style interiors.

Church of the Holy Sepulchre. The early church complex commissioned by Constantine (dedicated c. 335) in Jerusalem that incorporates the sites of Jesus' crucifixion and tomb/resurrection. In antiquity main areas included the *west-orientated *basilica-style Martyrium, the circular Anastasis (Gk. for "resurrection") over the tomb further to the west, and the Holy Garden courtyard (atrium) in-between connecting the two buildings. The Anastasis bore similarities to the sacred funerary buildings of pagan heroes, such as the implied tomb of Asclepius at Epidaurus, which too was a domed (conical) circular *tholos* supported by pillars (the burial place in the Anastasis is marked by a [nearly] central *octagonal entry into the ground, corresponding to the central circular pit of Asclepius's *tholos*).

The buildings of the Church of the Holy Sepulchre were later rebuilt and modified in the early Middle Ages (e.g., the basilica was now orientated toward the *east). The RC and a number of ECs maintain services there today.

In the case of Jesus, his *tomb* was also thought of as a *womb* (Col 1:18). Indeed, in the OT the earth is likened to a fertile mother (cf. Job 1:21; Is 26:19; the Edenic fount at Gen 2:10; cf. Germ. 3), and caves in antiquity were associated with divine birth (*see* Church of the Nativity). *See also* baptism.

Church of the Nativity. A *church building that stands over the traditional location of Jesus' birth. Originally begun during Constantine's reign and rebuilt in the sixth century, the church is orientated toward the *east, symbolic of birth. The place of birth was originally indicated by an *octagonal opening into the earthen grotto (divine births in antiquity being associated with the earth: Hesiod, *Theogony.* 477-484; *Homeric Hymn to Apollo* 113-122; Apollodorus, *Library* 2.4.1; Justin, *Dialogue with Trypho* 70; Germ. 3). *See also* font, baptismal.

ciborium. Latin meaning "a cup": (1) a container for the *consecrated *bread of the *Eucharist or (2) architecturally, a *baldachino-like structure.

Circumcision of Christ, Feast of the (January 1). A major feast, also called Holy Name (*EBCP*), held the eighth day (*octave) from *Christmas, and thus the day on which the circumcision of Jesus is remembered (cf. Gen 17:10-12; Lk 1:59). Color: white.

Cistercians. An ascetic RC monastic order (founded 1098). Historically they are connected with St. Bernard of Clairvaux and their early history coincides with the spread of *Gothic architecture.

clam shell. An ancient Christian implement used for the *baptism of children. *See also* apse; baptistery.

clerestory. An upper section (literally "clear story") in a *basilica or medieval *cathedral, incorporating a row of windows that runs parallel to the *nave.

clergy, cleric. *Ordained *minister or *priest; sometimes also used of the *religious, and thus those not strictly numbered among the *laity.

Cluniacs. An influential Benedictine group with a *monastery (founded tenth century) at Cluny, in Burgundy, France. The monastery, associated with the development of grand *Romanesque architecture, was destroyed during the French Revolution.

Codex Vaticanus. One of the earliest manuscripts of the Christian Bible, containing both New and Old Testaments in Greek (though the NT text breaks off after Heb 9:14). It is dated to the fourth century. Designated Codex B and housed in the Vatican Library, it is one of the most important copies of the NT. Its *lection divisions may be quite ancient (*see* Carrington, Philip). *See also* Septuagint.

collect. A fixed liturgical *prayer for a particular occasion (i.e., the prayer of the day), so called because it was the comprehensive prayer of the *minister that *collected* the prayers of others present. As some are quite ancient, collects encapsulate a tradition's theological reflection (*see* lex orandi, lex credendi). Many liturgical books provide the texts of numerous collects.

colors, liturgical. Colors prescribed for seasons and services.

Comes. Latin for "companion," in medieval parlance the *lectionary for *Mass.

Comfortable Words, The. In the *ABCP,* words said just before the *Liturgy of the Eucharist (but before the *offertory in the *EBCP*). They are composed of four passages of Scripture: Matthew 11:28, John 3:16, 1 Timothy 1:15 and 1 John 2:1-2.

commination. A threat of condemnation. *See* Communion exhortation.

Common of Saints. The prescribed liturgical *readings and *prayers *common* to those saints who do not have their own *proper (e.g., a *common* office for the apostles, or *common* office for martyrs).

Common Worship **(beg. 2000).** A series of volumes to supplement the *BCP* (1662) in the *Anglican Church. The purpose is to give a broader variety of forms to Anglican services, covering everything from *baptismal initiation to the *Daily Office, to even a Valentine's Day service.

communicant. One who partakes of the *Eucharist.

Communion. The English translation of Greek *koinōnia,* another name for the *Eucharist, especially for the actual distribution and eating of the bread and wine (*see* Liturgy of the Eucharist). World Communion Sunday is now recognized the first Sunday of October.

Communion exhortation. The words of admonishment in preparation for *Communion. Read at the beginning of the worship service or of the *Liturgy of the Eucharist, it is sometimes described as "fencing the table." It is especially prominent in the AC and P&RC.

Compline. Also known as Night Prayer, in the WC the last of the *Daily Office hours, occurring late at night before retiring (from Lat. *completus,* "complete"). It is analogous to Midnight Prayer in the EC. Typical recitations include Psalms 4, 31, 91 and 134 and the *Nunc Dimittis.

confession. From Latin *confessio,* meaning "acknowledgment." Historically, confession (Gk. *homologia*) is an oath agreeing to certain statements (e.g., Heb 3:1; 4:14; 10:23). Confessional statements of faith existed in the ancient church (Rom 1:3-4; 1 Jn 5:5; 1 Tim 6:13-14), perhaps connected with the baptismal *rite, as they remain to this day. Later statements of faith are also termed *confessions* (e.g., Belgic Confession; *Westminster Confession).

confession of sin. The penitent acknowledgment of sin. Confession of sin is most pointedly based on 1 John 1:9, which promises that those who confess their sins will be forgiven. In the liturgy, corporate confession of sin is usually said early in the worship service (followed immediately by *absolution) as preparation for the rest of the service. Involving reflection on the *Law in some Protestant churches, corporate confession has an additional leveling effect, establishing that all come as sinners to hear the *Word and receive the *sacrament. In some churches the act of corporate confession and absolution is called the Penitential *Rite/Order. Personal *examination* is an element of the *office of *Compline.

confirmation. A *rite that (re)affirms the *baptism (1) of one who now is of an age to knowingly and freely declare her or his faith after having been baptized as an infant (perhaps having now completed a period of *catechism) or (2) of one who was baptized in another tradition. The rite may also take place immediately after adult baptism (e.g., in the RC, where it is a *sacrament). The *laying on of hands is sometimes associated with confirmation. *See also* affirmation of faith; chrismation; sealing.

congregation. Those assembled for worship. Synonymous with *synagogue*.

congregational. A form of church government that is democratic (i.e., the congregation rather than a bishop or presbytery has ultimate ruling authority). The form of worship in the Congregational churches found in the United States is rooted in Puritan worship, which emphasized prayer, the *sermon and solemn reflection.

congregational prayer. *See* prayers of the people.

consecrate, consecration. To make something *holy; to set aside for holy purposes. *See* Epiclesis.

Consultation on Common Texts. A modern ecumenical organization that offers paradigmatic liturgical *readings and *forms that various denominations may share in, including the *Revised Common Lectionary*.

contemporary worship service. A modern corporate service that emphasizes informality, *praise music, a multimedia environment, and an eye toward the interests, entertainment and lexicon of younger generations. Its *formal roots are in the *revival service of worship. Key terms of purpose include "belonging" and "relevance." *See also* convergence service; seeker service; worship team.

convergence service. The mixing of traditional worship elements with *contemporary worship elements. *See also* ancient-future.

cope. From Latin *capa*, an outer garment sometimes worn by priests, somewhat like a *cape*. A *chasuble is similar.

Coptic Church. The historic Egyptian church, thriving today even outside of Egypt. The Coptic Orthodox Church is an ancient part of the EC that, while affirming the *Nicene Creed, does not agree to the christological formulation of the Council of Chalcedon (451). *Coptic* also refers to the Egyptian liturgical language of this church (both Coptic and Arabic are used in the services). Some important early versions of the NT are in Coptic, as well as the Gnostic library found at Nag Hammadi (Coptic translations of originally Greek texts). Historically, the Coptic *Rite has had a significant influence on the Ethiopian (Abyssinian) Church.

corporal. Derived from Latin *corpus*, "body," a white linen cloth laid on the *Communion *table and on which the *bread and *wine are placed. It is called the *corporal* to further identify the Communion elements with the body and blood of Jesus, which are themselves often covered by white cloths.

Corpus Christi, Feast of. A feast day commemorating the establishment of the *Eucharist. Celebrated the Thursday following *Trinity Sunday, the name is Latin for "Body of Christ." Instituted in the thirteenth century, it is held on a Thursday because the Eucharist itself was instituted on *Maundy Thursday. Color: white.

Council of Nicaea (325). The church council of bishops summoned by the emperor Constantine primarily to settle the issue of the divine nature of Jesus. The Arian Christians basically held that the Son was a lesser deity, not coeternal with the Father. The orthodox Christians, represented by, for example, Bishop Alexander of Alexandria and Athanasius, believed that the Son was of one substance with the Father and not created. The Council sided with the orthodox, composing the first form of what would become known as the *Nicene Creed.

Cranmer, Thomas (1489-1556). The *archbishop of Canterbury, English reformer and principal architect of the first and second prayer books of *Edward VI, laying the foundation for the *Book of Common Prayer*. Martyred at Oxford during the reign of Mary Tudor.

creation. An important aspect of Christian worship, as it was created by God, redeemed in Christ and sanctified in Christian worship. The Christian liturgical year is an affirmation of the goodness of creation as well as a reflection on life, death and rebirth. Modern endeavors, originally Enlightenment-based but now also market-driven and technology-enabled, to separate the life of the church from traditional worship patterns (both in time and space) engender a spirituality abstracted from creation. A "Season of Creation" is now recognized among some churches as part of the liturgical year (a series of five consecutive Sundays beginning with the first Sunday in September).

Credo. Latin for "I believe," part of the *Ordinary of the Latin *Mass. *See also* creed.

creed. From Latin *credo*, "I believe," a statement or *confession of belief (Lat. *symbolum*). Gathered Christians recite a creed to affirm their common faith, originally affirmed in their *baptisms. The recitation of a creed was part of the baptismal process in earlier times (the *redditio symboli*). An early affirmation of faith in the Bible begins the *Shema:* "Hear, O Israel: The LORD our God *is* one LORD" (Deut 6:4 KJV). *See also* Apostles' Creed.

Crosby, Fanny J. (1820-1915). An American poet, hymnist, evangelist and educator. Blind from infancy, Crosby's hymnic style greatly influenced other writers of *hymns, laying part of the foundation for what would become known as gospel music. Representative hymns: "Blessed Assurance," "To God Be the Glory."

cross. A torturous instrument of Roman execution and a *symbol of Christ's atoning death (Lat. *crux*; Gk. *stauros*). Crucifixion was a most reviled and shameful means of death for criminals (cf. Deut 21:23) but it became a symbol of Christianity due to the atoning death of Jesus on a Roman cross at Golgotha, outside of Jerusalem (Gal 3:13). In Christian symbolism the Latin cross has a longer vertical arm (✝) while the Greek cross has arms of equal length (✚). The use of the cross as a symbol was gradual, not to be found in the *catacombs except perhaps for the cross pattern of the *dome of heaven in the *cubicula* (perhaps making a connection with Jn 3:14; 8:28; 12:32).

Cross, Feast of the. An Eastern celebration of the *cross of Christ (September 14; c. September 27 in the *Coptic Church). Various feasts are associated with the cross of Christ in the WC, for example, The Invention of the Cross (May 3) and The Exaltation of the Cross (September 14 = *Holy Cross Day). *See also* Good Friday.

crucifer. In liturgical *procession, the one who carries the *cross.

crucifix. An image of Christ on the *cross, dating to the fifth century. Theologically, it demonstrates especially the WC's emphasis on Christ as the suffering savior.

cruciform. A term meaning "cross-shaped." Some Christian churches are cruciform, with the *transept forming the crossbeam in relation to the *nave. See the appendix.

cruet. A ceremonial pitcher to hold *Communion *wine and *water.

cult. A complex of religious forms and practices of worship or veneration (from Lat. *cultus*), a term broader in meaning than *liturgy.

cult of the Virgin. A significant medieval interest in the Virgin *Mary (beginning twelfth century, France) resulting in, among other things, dedication of *cathedrals to "Our Lady" (Fr. *Notre Dame*) and lay-oriented books for saying the Hours of the Virgin Mary (*see* Book of Hours).

curate. One who has the responsibility of the cure of souls (Lat. *cura*, "cure"), usually a *minister or *priest who assists the *rector.

D

Daily Office. Also known as the Divine Office or the Liturgy of the Hours (RC), a most important form of Christian liturgical worship, fulfilling the exhortation to "pray without ceasing" (1 Thess 5:17; cf. Acts 6:4; Eph 6:18). Precedence for regulated daily *prayer is found in the OT (Ps 5:3; 141:2; 119:62, 164; Dan 6:10), and evidence of regulated prayer among Christians is quite early (Acts 10:9; 16:25; cf. Tert., *Or.* 25).

The Daily Office is historically rooted in both the *cathedral prayers and the *monastic hours of prayer. Cathedral prayer was the public, *common prayer* service incorporating selected *psalms, *hymns and intercessory prayer (the *bishop giving the *collect), with services twice daily (morning and evening) as well as a weekly *vigil on Saturday evening. Cathedral hours at Jerusalem during the episcopacy of Cyril were observed and noted by the Spanish *nun Egeria in her *pilgrimage journal, an important historical document (c. late fourth century). Monastic prayer, in contrast, was far more frequent throughout the night and day, with emphasis on reciting the entire *Psalter in order (usually every week) and Scripture readings. Monastic prayer was far less public than cathedral prayer, and was even said privately at times. In the WC, the monastic office developed at Rome was enhanced and propagated by *Benedict. This office was divided into eight "hours": *Matins, *Lauds, Prime, Terce (9:00 a.m.), Sext (noon), None (3:00 p.m.), *Vespers and *Compline, with a number of these hours paralleled in *Apostolic Tradition* 41 (with reflections).

Over time these two forms of prayer—cathedral and monastic—influenced each other and thus various orders of prayer evolved within the various traditions of the EC and the WC. Significantly, during the Reformation *Cranmer collapsed content from the traditional offices into just two offices: Matins and Vespers.

Today in the WC Morning Prayer and Evening Prayer are the primary services (though the RC has retained most of the traditional offices) and have the following elements (though variations occur):

Opening versicle: e.g., "Lord, open our lips . . ." (Ps 51:15)
Gloria Patri
Invitatory Psalm
Hymn
Psalmody, appended with Gloria Patri
Scripture readings
Canticles, appended with Gloria Patri
Apostles' Creed
Kyrie Eleison
Lord's Prayer
Collect
Intercessory Prayer
Closing Prayers
Benedicamus
Benediction

A number of *liturgical books give the option of *confession of sin and *absolution at the beginning of an office. As part of *liturgical renewal, Noonday Prayer and Compline can now be found in many recent Protestant service books. *See also* Office of Readings. See Taft.

deacon. A church office literally meaning "servant" (Gk. *diakonos*). In the NT, the office of deacon arises in Acts 6:1-7. NT qualifications of the office are given at 1 Timothy 3:8-13, where women are likely not excluded from the office (1 Tim 3:11; cf. Rom 16:1). In the RC and LC the deacon is a trained layperson who assists the parish priest in the liturgical services (cf. *1 Clem.* 40, 41), and in a number of traditions reads the *Gospel. In other Protestant denominations the deacons handle the business affairs and maintenance needs of the local church (*stewards*). In some churches (e.g., Baptist) the deacons may have even more authority, functioning as *elders do in some denominations.

Decalogue. From Greek *deka*, "ten," and *logos*, "statement," another name for the *Ten Commandments (cf. Ex 34:28 LXX).

December 13. *See* Lucia, Feast of St.

decision. In the *revival service of worship, the faith-action on the part of the listener to "accept Christ" or, if already a Christian, to rededicate one's life, often involving the physical act of responding to an *altar call.

declaration of forgiveness. A statement of forgiveness following the *confession of sin in the worship service. It approximates *absolution, but vests authority in the *minister only to inform or remind the congregants that they are forgiven rather than vesting the minister with actual authority to forgive.

dedication, infant. *See* baby dedication.

deiknymena. A Greek term meaning "things explained, brought forth." In ancient Greek religion it is often the culmination of a ritual process following the *legomena* and *drōmena.* *Mystagogy fulfills a similar role in Christianity, and the Christian *homily or *sermon is analogous, being the exegesis of the sacred words and actions.

Deus Misereatur. Latin for "God, be compassionate [to us]," the first words of Psalm 67, sometimes recited at *Evening Prayer.

Diatessaron. From Greek, meaning "by means of four," a harmony of the *Gospel narratives constructed from the four canonical Gospels by Tatian, a one-time student of Justin Martyr. It was for a time the liturgical version of the Gospels used in *Syrian churches.

Didache. Greek for "Teaching [of the Twelve Apostles]" and among the earliest postapostolic writings (parts perhaps predating some NT writings). A composite work that developed over time (first to second centuries), it is the earliest presentation of a *formal Christian liturgy, including baptism (chaps. 7, 9) and the Eucharist (chaps. 9-10, 14). Likely produced in *Syria and written in Greek, it influenced later church *orders.

Didascalia Apostolorum. Meaning "Teaching of the Apostles," an early Christian *order (c. first half of third century, *Syria), originally written in Greek but mainly surviving in Syriac and Latin. It was influenced by the *Didache*.

Dignus Es. A *canticle (Lat. "You are worthy") based on songs of adoration in *Revelation (4:11; 5:9-10, 13). Also known as *Glory and Honor* (CW).

diptychs. An intercessory *prayer section in the *Liturgy of the Eucharist that focuses on specific believers, both deceased and living.

disciplina arcani. Latin for "the rule of secrecy," a term describing the ancient church restriction against revealing certain particulars of the faith to those outside the faith. For example, the *Apostles' Creed was forbidden to be communicated even to catechumens until the eve of their *baptism (Cyr., *Procatech*. 12, where the creed is termed a *mystery*). Such a restriction may also have applied to the *Lord's Prayer and the *Twenty-third Psalm. The *disciplina arcani* is analogous to the severe demand in antiquity that what was spoken or done in a *mystery cult must not be revealed.

discipline. The third "mark" of a true church in the Calvinist tradition (preaching the *Word and rightly administering the *sacraments being the first two). Discipline within the P&RC is most apparent at *Communion, access to which may be denied to Christians under discipline.

dismissal. The exhortation or charge near the end of the worship service instructing the congregation to live out the good news in their daily lives. It is from this that the term *Mass* derives (from Lat. *Missa*, derived from *mitto*, "to send").

Divine Liturgy. Another name for the *Eucharist (EC).

Divine Office. *See* Daily Office.

Dix, Gregory (1901-1952). An *Anglican scholar whose influential

The Shape of the Liturgy (1945) advocated historical continuity of the liturgical tradition within Christianity, especially with regard to the *Eucharist. He also edited an important English translation (with commentary) of the *Apostolic Tradition*.

do ut des. A Latin expression meaning "I give in order that you may give"; the basis of votive offerings.

dome. A semispherical architectural form implying the dome of the heavenlies, partially rooted in the Near East and popularized through the influence of Greco-Roman architecture. Many domes in the ancient world were likely wooden and therefore have perished. The concrete dome of the Pantheon in Rome survives, a temple to "all the gods" built during the reign of Hadrian (c. A.D. 120; dedicated as a Christian church in 609), and significant domes built since have been influenced by it, for example, *Hagia Sophia, Florence Cathedral (by Filippo Brunelleschi, dedicated 1436), *St. Peter's, Rome, *St. Paul's, London, and the U.S. Capitol in Washington, D.C. (by Thomas Walter, 1863). The interior of the Pantheon contains seven niches for statues of the gods representing the seven planets reckoned at the time (i.e., Sun, Moon, Mercury, Venus, Mars, Jupiter and Saturn). The dome's interior was formerly decorated with stars, and the thirty-foot-diameter opening in the middle of the dome represented the divine all-seeing eye (Lat. *oculus*). In Byzantine architecture, the pendentive adapted the circular dome to a rectangular building.

dome of heaven. An ancient ceiling motif explicated in the famous study by Karl Lehmann. With the ancient *dome as an undergirding conceptual theme, it conceives the heavens as a canopy orientated to four corners (cf. Is 40:22), often with a primary deity at the center (*see* Pantocrator). A motif in Roman palaces (cf. Eusebius, *Life of Constantine* 3.49), baths and funerary settings, it was also common in the *cubicula* of the Christian Roman *catacombs, where Jesus was portrayed in the center ring as the *Good Shepherd, and later portrayed in Byzantine domes as the Pantocrator. An early extant pagan version of the dome of heaven has Sirens at the corners (Etruscan, fifth century B.C.), and indeed Christian art first had winged figures at the four corners, especially birds, and later the winged *Evangelists (influenced by Ezek 10:14; Rev 4:7).

Even in pre-Christian times a cross pattern emerged within the motif, a pattern meaningfully continued by Christians. The halo-circumscribed cross of the Byzantine Pantocrator may be influenced by this cosmic motif. The dome of heaven was frequently adapted to semicircular *apsidal architecture within churches, as it was previously in pagan buildings, for example in basilicas of Roman emperors as well as the focal *iconography of *mithraea*. Dome of heaven imagery may be invoked in Peter's vision (Acts 10:11-12) and the description of the coming of the Son of Man (Mt 24:30-31).

dove. The *symbol of the *Holy Spirit, who descended "like a dove on" Jesus at his *baptism (Mk 1:10 par.). As the Holy Spirit is closely associated with baptismal new birth (Jn 3:5), so the dove imagery is associated with (re)creation/(re)birth in the Bible: the dove-like hovering of the Spirit of God at creation (Gen 1:2); the dove with the olive branch after the flood (Gen 8:10-11); and Jesus' baptism and the coming of the kingdom of God (Mk 1:10, 14-15). A symbol of life and the life-giving Holy Spirit, the dove is a prominent symbol in the funerary art of the Roman Christian *catacombs.

In the ancient Near East, the dove was the primary symbol of the mother goddess (e.g., Ishtar, Astarte, Atargatis, Greco-Roman Aphrodite/Venus; cf. Virgil, *Aeneid* 6.193), symbolic of life and fertility/birth. The Hebrew word for *spirit* is feminine (Heb. *rûaḥ*; Gk. *pneuma* is neuter; Lat. *spiritus* is masculine), and thus the Holy Spirit can take feminine pronouns in, for example, *Ephrem's *hymns.

doxology. From Greek *doxa*, "glory," a *hymn of praise. The greater doxology is the *Gloria in Excelsis Deo, the lesser doxology the *Gloria Patri. One of the most famous doxologies, set to the "Old 100th" *hymn tune by Louis Bourgeois of Calvin's Geneva, is that of Thomas Ken: "Praise God, from whom all blessings flow; Praise Him, all creatures here below; Praise Him above, ye heav'nly host: Praise Father, Son, and Holy Ghost. Amen."

Doxologies in Scripture include 1 Chronicles 16:36; 29:10; Daniel 2:20; Psalm 134 (concluding the *Psalms of Ascent); Romans 9:5; 11:36; 16:27; 2 Corinthians 11:31; 1 Timothy 1:17; 1 Peter 1:3; and Revelation 5:12. See also the traditional ending of the *Lord's Prayer.

drama. A sketch or longer dramatic presentation incorporated into a *contemporary worship service, often offering a real-life illustration of the theme of the *sermon. In this its goal is not unlike a medieval *morality play, though the latter was not performed within the worship service. *See also* liturgical drama.

drōmena. A Greek term meaning "things that are done," in ancient Greek religion those actions performed in *cult, loosely corresponding to the English term *ritual*. It is from the same Greek root (*draō*) as *drama*.

Dura-Europos, church building of. A highly significant *domus ecclesiae* ("house of the church") that is the earliest extant Christian house of worship (c. mid-third century) and the best verifiable one from before the time of Constantine (see Kraeling for in-depth description). It was a home that was converted to a place of worship, a development beyond the earliest Christian corporate worship that took place often within private homes and was overseen by certain households ("house churches"; Acts 2:46; 12:12; 20:8; 1 Cor 16.15, 19; Col 4:15; 1 Thess 5:12; Philem 1-2; Justin, *Dial*. 47.2), a general practice of private cults in Roman times that often were run or funded by patrons in domestic settings (e.g., synagogues and *mithraea*; see L. Michael White).

The most significant part of the Dura-Europos building was the *baptistery, with its *sarcophagus-like baptismal *font at the *western wall of the room and a *baldachino-like pillared canopy. The underside of the canopy above the font was painted a deep blue background covered with eight-pointed stars, as was the whole of the ceiling of the baptistery (fragments of a *moon were also discovered) (see Kraeling). *Apse-like on the western wall above the font was a semicircular area containing the image of the *Good Shepherd (smaller and fainter is a drawing of Adam and Eve; cf. *Gospel of Thomas* 37), content and arrangement quite similar to the *funerary* art in the semicircular area above the entrance to Galla Placidia's mausoleum in *Ravenna (*see also* dome of heaven). Though seriously damaged in some places, the rest of the walls in the baptistery have representations of Jesus walking on the water, the healing of the paralytic, the woman at the well, David and Goliath and, near the font, a tomb with women approaching with torches. Some of these themes are known from Christian funerary art (*see* catacombs, Christian Roman).

E

east. The cardinal point (east = Gk. *anatolē*; cf. Mt 2:1-2) of the compass associated with the rising of the sun (cf. Gk. text at Rev 7:2), and thus dawn (cf. Bar 4:36). It is *symbolic of resurrection, Jesus rising on *Sunday morning, the Christians' victorious sun (*sol invictus*; cf. Ezek 43:1-4; Zech 6:12 LXX) and also foreshadows the hope of his second coming (Mt 24:27; Germ. 11). Traditionally churches, and thus their corporate worship, are orientated toward the east (i.e., the *altar at the eastern end of the building).

Easter, date of. Generally speaking, falls on the first *Sunday following the first full moon on or after the spring equinox, but historically has been specifically predetermined according to certain calculations. A discrepancy between EC and WC dating of Easter is due to the introduction of the *Gregorian calendar in the West in 1582 and is considered an obstacle to unity within the body of Christ (F&O 11).

Easter (Sunday of the Resurrection). The ancient major feast celebrating Jesus' resurrection from the dead on *Sunday morning following his crucifixion and burial. Traditionally Easter is celebrated through *Pentecost (*see* Eastertide). The name *Easter* is perhaps based on the name of a goddess (Anglo-Saxon *Eastre*) who was celebrated in the month of April, or it might be derived from some Germanic term for "east" or "dawn" (see Adam). Color: white.

Easter Vigil. *See* Paschal Vigil.

Eastern churches. Those churches whose *rites and/or theological distinctives are rooted in the ancient churches of the eastern Mediterranean and Middle East, and include many of the historical churches of eastern Europe. They tend to be more traditionally liturgical. While the historical trend in the West has been an emphasis on Mark's suffering Son of Man (and thus crucifixes), in the East it has been as much on John's exalted One and movement toward this One (Jn 12:32), with the church building emphasizing (vertically) the meeting place of heaven and earth, as it was with ancient Near Eastern temples.

Eastertide. The fifty-day period of joy beginning on *Easter and ending at *Pentecost (Tert., *Bapt.* 19). Christ's death and resurrection, celebration of the *Eucharist, and post-baptismal instruction (*mystagogy) are emphasized during this period. *Readings from the Gospel of John and the book of Acts are traditional. In antiquity this period was referred to as *Pentecost. Color: white.

Ecumenical Creeds. From Latin *oecumenicus,* "universal," the three *creeds known as the *Apostles', the *Nicene and the *Athanasian.

Edward VI (1537-1553). A king of England, son of Henry VIII and brother of Mary Tudor and Elizabeth I. Edward was a Protestant and, as part of his religious reforms, was instrumental in the production of two editions of a prayer book (now named after him). These prayer books are considered the first (1549) and second (1552) editions of the *ABCP.*

elder. Cognate to "older," in many Protestant denominations a *lay authority within local church governance. The English word often translates the Greek *presbyteros* in the NT (1 Tim 4:14). *See also* priest.

Ember Days. From Anglo-Saxon *ymbryne,* "circuit," a set of three days occurring four times each year. The set days are Wednesday, Friday and Saturday (in that order), and these sets occur after *December 13, *Ash Wednesday, *Whitsunday (*Pentecost) and *Holy Cross Day (sometimes as a harvest celebration). These days are set aside for *fasting, and their observance dates back to Rome in the early third century. They are perhaps pagan in origin, connected with the agricultural cycle. Nonetheless, certain churches have attached functions to their recognition, especially *ordinations. Color: red.

Entrance, Great, and Little Entrance. *See* procession.

Ephphatha. Aramaic for "Be opened," a command given by Jesus when healing a blind man (Mk 7:34). The use of the expression in initiatory rites in the WC is quite ancient. In the OC this pericope is the Gospel *lesson for the fourth Saturday in Lent.

Ephrem, St. An influential fourth-century *Syrian hymnist and biblical commentator. Importantly, his work reflects a more Semitic sensibility of Christian *symbol and worship.

Epiclesis. A Greek *cultic term *(epiklēsis)* for the prayerful "invocation" of a deity, that is, the calling forth of a deity to be present, to "come" to various occasions (e.g., a *litany of requests or a *sacrifice; see Laager). It is an important part of the *Liturgy of the Eucharist, where the presence of the Holy Spirit is requested to *consecrate the *bread and *wine (especially in the EC), even making Christ present (or substantiated) at the *altar (Cyr., *Myst. Cat.* 5.7; CCC 1105-7; 1353). Aside from the cultural milieu, the impetus for the eucharistic *epiclesis* is perhaps reflected at Hebrews 9:14 (cf. Rom 15:16; see Laager). Ancient eucharistic *epicleseis* include *Didache* 10.6 ("Maranatha," Aram. meaning "Our Lord, come!"), *Apostolic Tradition* 4.12 and possibly the first *petition of the *Lord's Prayer. Another possible *epiclesis* is "Amen. Come, Lord Jesus!" (Rev 22:20), a text that is part of the Eucharistic Prayer in some liturgical settings.

Epiphany, Feast of the (January 6). A major feast, known in the OC as Theophany. The Greek word *epiphaneia* means "manifestation," and observance became widespread by the late fourth century. It has been closely associated with the *baptism of Jesus, where Jesus as the Son of God is first made *manifest* (Mk 1:11). January 6 was also the date for celebrating the birth of Jesus in certain EC (to this day in the Armenian Church), and early on it was closely associated with the incarnation. Indeed, some have seen in Jesus' baptism a kind of birth (note the textual variant at Lk 3:22: "today I have begotten you"; cf. Heb 1:5; 5:5, rooted in Ps 2:7; cf. *Gospel of the Ebionites* 3; *Gospel of the Hebrews* 2-3). With its commemoration of the baptism of Jesus, it is no surprise that Epiphany is popular for baptism of new Christians (dating back to the fourth century). Interestingly, whereas *Christmas originated in the WC and spread to the EC, Epiphany developed first in the EC and spread to the WC. The WC tends to commemorate the arrival of the Magi on this day. Generally the RC and some other WC now commemorate the *Baptism of Our Lord on the Sunday after Epiphany is commemorated. The Cana wedding miracle (Jn 2:1-12) is also commemorated on January 6. Color: white.

episcopal. Those churches or ecclesiastical territories governed by a *bishop.

equinox. From Latin meaning "equal night," the two days in the year when, regardless of one's latitude on the earth's surface, the length of day and night are equal due to the sun's location (i.e., crossing the celestial equator). These two days are the spring equinox (March 20/21) and the autumnal equinox (September 22/23), beginning spring and autumn respectively. The spring equinox is fundamental to setting the date of *Easter.

Eucharist. Traditionally the paramount *rite of the Christian community and, when celebrated, the goal and apex of Christian *Sunday worship. From Greek *eucharistia*, "thanksgiving" (e.g., 1 Cor 10:16: the cup of thanksgiving; cf. 11:24), it's the name for the Christian rite of *Communion, clearly so designated as early as *Didache* 9.1. The Eucharist, also known as the Lord's Supper or the Table of the Lord, is a *sacrament (or *ordinance) of the church, a rite instituted by Jesus himself as the new covenant (Mk 14:22-26; Mt 26:26-29; Lk 22:14-20; 1 Cor 11:23-25). The Eucharist involves the ceremonial eating of *bread and drinking of *wine, elements Jesus equated with his flesh and blood (Jn 6:53; Ign., *Rom.* 7.3) given for the forgiveness of sins (Mt 26:28), a participation in (*koinōnia*) Jesus' blood and body (1 Cor 10:16) given in his death (1 Cor 11:26). Preference for a fixed *form of eucharistic celebration is found as early as *1 Clement* 41. Banquets are a common motif in Christian *catacomb art.

An important part of Christian corporate worship (1 Cor 11:26; *see* Liturgy of the Eucharist), the Eucharist is variously interpreted. Historically, it is the sacrament of sustenance, the manna for the life journey of the body of Christ (Jn 6:31-33, 48-51); the ongoing redemptive work of God as Christ's flesh and blood are extended to the believer for eternal sustenance (Iren., *Haer.* 5.2.2-3), the medicine of immortality (Ign., *Eph.* 20.2), the receiving of and union with Christ (1 Cor 10:16; cf. Mk 8:14, 16-17), as well as union with his corporate body of the saints (1 Cor 10:16-17). Eschatologically, it is a foretaste of the heavenly banquet (Lk 22:30; Heb 6:5). Recognized OT *types include Melchizedek (Gen 14:18; Heb 6:20; 7:1-3), the manna from heaven (Ex 16:4; Jn 6:32; 1 Cor 10:3), and Moses and the water from the rock (Ex 17:6; 1 Cor 10:4).

As Jesus' death on the cross was a *sacrifice for sin, some understand the Eucharist as a sacrifice (1 Cor 11:24-26; Justin, *Dial.* 41; perhaps *Did.* 14.1; Iren., *Haer.* 4.18.4-5), the historical event of

Christ's atonement made present (cf. LG 3; CCC 1364, 1367); not a resacrifice, but the one final sacrifice (Heb 7:27) made present (CCC 1366-67; see Anamnesis; sacred time). Lutherans and some other Protestants recognize Jesus as physically present, but not as a sacrifice, and *transubstantiation is not implied. Others tend to interpret the Eucharist in a spiritual or *symbolic way, recognizing no physical presence of Jesus in/with the elements yet still communicating God's grace (see real presence), while still others see only a memorial of Christ's atonement and God's grace, and perhaps an occasion for moral resolve.

The earliest written formulation of the eucharistic rite we have is that of Paul (1 Cor 11:23-26), demonstrating that the *Last Supper of Jesus was intricately connected with the liturgy of the early church. This celebration of the Eucharist was closely tied to Jesus' death as sacrifice (1 Cor 10:16-21). Indeed, the *tradition* that Paul received and passed on is primarily the death and resurrection of Jesus Christ (1 Cor 15:3-8), memorialized and played out in the celebration of the Eucharist (1 Cor 11:23; cf. 10:16-17). This is Paul's gospel (1 Cor 15:1-4). Other early texts concerning the eucharistic liturgy include *Didache* 9-10, 14 and Justin, *1 Apol*. 65-67.

Modern scholarship has noted that references to Christ's body and blood are absent in certain early liturgies (e.g., the *Did*.). Thus some scholars note other primitive Christian ritual meals that lack Last Supper meanings, with variations including a cup-bread sequence, bread and water as the elements, or bread only (see Bradshaw [c]).

Frequency of celebrating Communion varies greatly, with some churches celebrating weekly (e.g., Disciples of Christ) or more frequently (e.g., RC and AC), while some celebrate only monthly or even a few times per year (four times per year has been common among the P&RC since *Zwingli). Frequency tends to be factored by theological understanding, logistics for preparation and target constituency of the congregation. In the Middle Ages only the bread was distributed to the communicants in the WC. The Reformation guaranteed participation in "both kinds," in other words, both bread and wine to be given to the *communicants. In the OC the congregants usually receive the bread called *antidoron* at the end of the service.

Admittance to participate in the Eucharist is along a spectrum. Generally speaking, some churches celebrate *closed Communion* (only those belonging to the particular church or denomination), some *close Communion* (e.g., only those with whom the church has denominational ecclesiastical fellowship) and some *open Communion* (all professing Christians). Traditionally the Eucharist is not given to the unbaptized (*Did.* 9.5; Justin, *1 Apol.* 65, 66; cf. *Ap. Trad.* 37), with Paul's warning being paramount (1 Cor 11:27), and may be denied to some believers as a matter of *discipline ("fencing the table" in the P&RC). In the OC the Eucharist is extended to baptized infants.

A number of traditions, due to conscience, recovering alcoholism and the participation of children, substitute grape juice for wine. Such traditions include Wesleyan, Restoration, Holiness and Adventist churches. Other churches, though primarily celebrating with wine, provide the option of grape juice. In the ancient church the eucharistic wine was mixed with water (Justin, *1 Apol.* 62; cf. Jn 19:34). Confessional statements: Aug. Conf. 10; Heid. Cat. 75-82; West. Conf. 29; BF&M 7; CCC 1322-1419. *See also* agape; Aberkios Inscription; Eucharistic Prayer; fish.

Eucharistic Prayer. The Prayer of Consecration in the *Liturgy of the Eucharist, sometimes called the "great thanksgiving," which praises and supplicates God based on God's great acts of creation and redemption. Although some include under the term both the *Preface and Prayer of Consecration, specifically the Eucharistic Prayer follows the *Sanctus and includes the *Words of Institution, the *Anamnesis and the *Epiclesis (the *Lord's Prayer may also be included). In the RC it is called the *Canon of the Mass*, the traditional *rite little changed since the time of Ambrose, although the WC is expanding its repertoire of variations.

Euchologion. Greek for "prayer book," the *liturgical book of the EC with *forms for both the *Divine Liturgy and the *Daily Office.

evangelist. (1) Someone who proclaims the gospel (Gk. *euangelion*; Lat. *evangelium*, "good news"). In modern parlance it refers to those appointed for proclaiming the gospel with the intention of making converts. (2) An author of one of the four canonical Gospels, in other words, Matthew, Mark, Luke and John. These four are represented in Christian art by a man, lion, ox and eagle, respectively (cf. Ezek 10:14; Rev 4:7; Germ. 32). These four figures, usually winged, are often found at the four corners of a *dome of heaven motif.

eve. An evening observance prior to the day of a feast. Based on the Jewish reckoning of beginning the religious day the previous evening, the *eve* of a feast begins around sunset the day before. For example, the *office for the *eve* of Epiphany (January 5) begins the feast of Epiphany (January 6). *Eves* of major feasts are characterized by *abstinence.

Evening Prayer. Also known as *Vespers, the office said in the evening (*see* Daily Office). As the *Psalter forms the core of the Daily Office, historically and generally Psalm 141 (140) in the EC and Psalm 104:19-23 in the WC are especially recited at Evening Prayer (see Bradshaw [B]). Evening psalms in the AC include 98 (Cantate Domino) and 67 (*Deus Misereatur). Appropriate *canticles are the *Magnificat and *Nunc Dimittis.

Evensong. *See* Vespers; Evening Prayer.

ewer. A pitcher for water.

exhortation. The addressing of the conscience. Before the *Eucharist there may be an exhortation to examine oneself, as Paul directs (1 Cor 11:28).

exorcism. The *rite renouncing the works of the devil. It has been a common rite from earliest Christianity (cf. Mk 3:11; 5:7; see Kelly), often part of prebaptismal preparation, along with *prayer and *fasting (*Ap. Trad.* 20.7; Cyr., *Procatech.* 13; 14).

Eyck, Jan van (early fifteenth century). A major painter of the northern Renaissance, famous for the polyptych known as the *Ghent Altarpiece*, a reflection on the *Lamb of the book of *Revelation.

F

fair linen. A fine linen cloth that covers the Communion table, overhanging lengthwise, often incorporating five *crosses in the fabric's design representing the five wounds Jesus endured on the cross. Traditionally the fair linen represents Jesus' burial cloth (cf. Mk 15:46; Jn 19:40).

fast. Day or period of *abstinence, often for solemn reflection. In the ancient church, and still today in the OC, Wednesday and Friday were fasts (*Did.* 8); now only Friday is recognized as such in the WC.

Father, God the. First person of the Holy *Trinity. Traditionally, the person of the Trinity to whom prayer is most often addressed in corporate worship (Rom 15:6; Gal 4:6; Eph 3:14; 5:20; 1 Pet 1:17; the *Lord's Prayer).

feast. From Latin *festum*, "festival," which is from Latin *festus*, "joyful."

feast day. A day set aside for honoring some person or event. Significant honorees and events include Apostle Andrew (November 30); Confession of Peter (January 18, *EBCP*); Conversion of Paul (January 25); Matthias (February 24; May 14); Joseph of Nazareth (March 19); Mark the Evangelist (April 25); Apostles Philip and James the Less (May 1); Philip the Deacon (June 6); Barnabas (June 11); Apostles Peter and Paul (June 29); Mary Magdalene (July 22); Apostle James (July 25; April 30); Virgin Mary (August 15); Apostle Bartholomew (August 24); Apostle Matthew (September 21); Michael and the Angels (September 29); Luke the Evangelist (October 18); James the Just (October 23); Apostles Simon and Jude (October 28); Apostle Thomas (December 21; July 3); Stephen the Deacon (December 26); Apostle John (December 27).

feria. A calendar day (apart from Saturdays and Sundays) that has no specially assigned religious observance.

festival. *See* feast.

fish. An ancient Christian symbol. Fish figure prominently in the *Gospel narratives, with a number of the original disciples being fishermen (Mt 4:18-22) and fish being used in parables and other lessons (Mt 7:10; 13:47; 17:27). In ancient Christian symbolism the fish usually refers to Jesus (*see* ΙΧΘΥΣ) and thus is present in Christian *iconography (e.g., the *catacombs). Because they were born of the waters of *baptism, Christians could be thought of as "little fish," following in the manner of Jesus, the ΙΧΘΥΣ (Tert., *Bapt.* 1).

Representations of banquet meals in ancient Christian catacomb art include fish, perhaps anticipated in the linguistic and conceptual parallels between the Gospel feeding stories and the *Last Supper (Mk 6:32-44; 8:1-9; 14:22-25; Jn 6:4-14; cf. Augustine, *Confessions* 13.21; *see also* bread). Even among ancient pagan tombs there are representations of fish, an obvious symbol of life and fertility, and often associated with Near Eastern mother goddesses (especially *Syrian). It was likely at times a meal for the dead. In fact, the multiplication of the loaves and fish has a distinct aspect of the chthonic and of fecundity about it (*see* hero cult). *See also* Aberkios Inscription.

flowers. Expressions of God's *creation and *symbolic of Jesus Christ's resurrection and the new life communicated to believers. Living or fresh flowers are often placed on the *Communion *table.

font, baptismal. A container holding baptismal water, whether within a *baptistery or a church interior (in medieval times becoming located at the *west end of the church building). In earlier times, as was the case with baptisteries, their shape varied (e.g., rectangular, hexagonal, *cruciform). These shapes had *symbolic meaning, usually of the funerary kind, and even today these shapes may be utilized for fonts, even if they are of the more portable type. Since Christian *baptism is both burial (Rom 6:3) and rebirth (Titus 3:5), the font is considered the womb of the church. From it emerge the born-again believers, born of water (Jn 3:3, 5; Cyr., *Myst. Cat.* 2.4). This concept is echoed throughout the writings of ancient Christians, with Cyprian famously stating that God cannot be one's Father if the church is not one's mother (*The Unity of the Catholic Church* 4; cf. Cyr., *Procatech.* 13).

foot washing. A ritual found regularly among certain Anabaptist and Brethren groups, though occasional observance can be found among other groups. Since Jesus' washing of the disciples' feet took place around the time of the *Last Supper (Jn 13:1-11), foot washing today may take place in conjunction with the celebration of *Communion.

form. A set way of procedure (thus *formal* and *formality*). A *form* of worship is a traditional pattern of worship. Though form may become restrictive, it also provides for what is essential, *style* providing freedom of expression and creativity within form. Even for those traditions that enjoy a certain amount of *spontaneity in worship, a general form maintains order, the antithesis of chaos (cf. Gen 1:2). Not to be confused with *formulaic*, which is an aspect of mechanistic expediency. *See also* rite.

Fraction. *See* Breaking of the Bread.

frontlet, frontal. A decorative outer cloth on the *Communion table.

funerary rites. Religious services for the deceased. The church has always taken care of its own (e.g., *catacomb *loculi*; *Ap. Trad.* 40), and thus many *liturgical books provide *forms for funerary services. Color: purple, black or white (the latter especially in the case of children).

G

Gabrieli, Giovanni (c. 1555-1612). A major composer of music (both sacred and secular) and an organist based at *St. Mark's Cathedral, Venice. Trained by his uncle Andrea Gabrieli, who in turn was trained by Adriaan Willaert (both also at St. Mark's), he continued the great and developing musical tradition of that *cathedral.

Gallican Rite. An important ancient *rite of Gaul (France) that had influence on other WC liturgies.

gathering rites. Elements of the worship service that take place at the beginning, from the *call to worship to the *collect. *See* order of worship.

General Thanksgiving. A famous prayer composed by *Cranmer for the final part of the *BCP* *Daily Office.

Geneva liturgy. The order of worship *Calvin brought to Geneva after spending time with Martin Bucer at Strasbourg. It was the basis for John Knox's *Genevan Service Book* (1556) that influenced the Scottish Presbyterian order of worship.

George, Feast of Saint (April 23). A feast day since the early fourth century, the celebration of a Christian martyr whose tomb is at Lydda (modern Lod, Israel). Celebrated in the EC, Saint George is the patron saint of England and mythic slayer of the dragon.

Germanus, St. (c. 640-733). The patriarch of Constantinople to whom is attributed a valuable commentary on the *Byzantine liturgy of his time.

gesture. A meaningful bodily action that takes place in the worship service (e.g., *standing, *kneeling, the *sign of the cross, bowing, and the raising of *hands).

Gloria in Excelsis Deo. A *hymn also known as the Greater Gloria, part of the *Ordinary of the Latin *Mass. The hymn begins with Luke 2:14, the song the angels sang at Christ's birth. As it is a joyful hymn, many liturgies omit it during the penitential seasons of *Advent and *Lent. Its use in the liturgy is ancient (originally composed in Greek). In the EC it is part of *Matins. A famous setting is by Vivaldi (in D major); more recently a contemporary *praise music variation was composed by Rick Founds and Bill Batstone as "We Praise You for Your Glory." The *EBCP* gives the following wording:

Glory to God in the highest,
    and peace to his people on earth.

Lord God, heavenly King,
almighty God and Father,
    we worship you, we give you thanks,
    we praise you for your glory.

Lord Jesus Christ, only Son of the Father,
Lord God, Lamb of God,
you take away the sin of the world:
    have mercy on us;
you are seated at the right hand of the Father:
    receive our prayer.

For you alone are the Holy One,
you alone are the Lord,
you alone are the Most High,
    Jesus Christ,
    with the Holy Spirit,
    in the glory of God the Father. Amen. (*EBCP*, Holy Eucharist II)

Gloria Patri. Latin for "Glory to the Father," an ancient *trinitarian *hymn of adoration (fourth century): "Glory to the Father, and to the Son, and to the Holy Spirit: as it was in the beginning, is now, and will be for ever. Amen" (*EBCP*).

glory. In Greek, *doxa*, referring to God's radiant splendor.

godparent. A church member or other baptized Christian who serves as spiritual adviser to a child presented for *baptism, vouching as well for the conduct and life of the child's parents. *See also* sponsor.

God's greeting. The welcoming of the worshipers, spoken by the *minister. For example: "Grace to you and peace from God our Father and the Lord Jesus Christ" (Phil 1:2, *EBCP*; cf. 2 Cor 13:13; Eph 1:2; Jn 20:21).

golden calf. The object of worship erected by the newly freed children of Israel while they awaited Moses' return from Mt. Sinai (Ex 32:4; 1 Kings 12:28). The calf was meant to be a focal point for worship of God (Ex 32:5), and thus it has become synonymous with sincere but wrongly informed worship (cf. Gen 4:3-5; Heb 11:4; 1 Cor 11:27-30).

golden number. Also known as Prime, the number used to determine the date of Easter for any particular year. The *BCP* gives the rule for finding the golden number. It is rooted in the nineteen-year lunar-solar cycle of the Greek astronomer Meton (432 B.C.), the reconciliation of the solar and lunar cycles, in other words, the reunion of sun and moon. The discovery of the time period was of astronomical and mythic importance to the ancients, and even Homer's *Odyssey* may incorporate something like this cycle as a subtheme manifested in Odysseus's reunion with Penelope.

Good Friday. A major holy day, the Friday of *Holy Week, memorializing the death of Jesus. The most solemn day of the Christian *calendar, it is the Friday on which Jesus was crucified and died for the sins of the world. Variations of worship abound, even among churches with strong liturgical traditions, partially because aspects of *Maundy Thursday are collapsed into this day in numerous churches. Traditionally it is a *fast, with celebration of the *Eucharist omitted in some Protestant services and *sanctuary crosses draped in black. The service usually takes place any time from noon on. Good Friday appears not to have been commemorated until the fourth century (Jerusalem), as the earlier church appears to have begun the solemn part of the *Pascha with the Easter *Vigil on Saturday evening, which was solemn until midnight and joyous thereafter (see Adam). Color: black and/or red.

Good Shepherd. An image of Jesus with a ram or lamb over his shoulders (Gk. *kriophoros*) or surrounded by a flock or both. The form is pagan in background (e.g., Hermes), but early on Christians represented Jesus as such, based on Scripture (Jn 10:11; Mt 9:36; 25:32; 26:31; Heb 13:20; 1 Pet 2:25; 5:4; Ps 23:1). It is found as the backdrop in the *baptistery *font of the church building at *Dura-Europos, and also in *dome of heaven motifs in the Roman *catacombs (*see* Pantocrator), both being contexts of funerary significance.

gospel songs. Mostly American songs for corporate worship, distinguishable from *hymns in that they are more personal or emotive in nature (emphasis on religion of the "heart"). Formally, where hymns are composed mainly of verses, gospel songs tend to emphasize refrains. Frequently expressing personal commitment and faith in God, they are less theological than hymns, though there is an emphasis on the cross and blood atonement. Their emergence is linked historically with the nineteenth-century *revival service of worship. Indeed, many famous songs were originally associated with revivalists. "Southern gospel" is one branch. Representative songs: "Blessed Assurance," "I Love to Tell the Story," "In the Garden." *See also* African American spirituals.

Gospel(s). The first four books of the NT that tell the sacred story of Jesus. From early times these books formed the core of Christian liturgical Scripture. In the *Liturgy of the Word the Gospel is the final *lesson, and the congregation is usually standing. It is Jesus who speaks in the Gospel lesson, and thus, for example, the singing of John 6:68 may precede the reading (LC). *See also* evangelist.

Gothic cathedrals. The *cathedrals of the High and Late Middle Ages. Developed from the *Romanesque *basilica, they were characterized by *rose windows, flying buttresses and pointed arches. The latter's weight-directing ability allowed these churches to attain great heights and to incorporate many stained-glass windows. Since the cathedral was the seat of a *bishop, and thus urban in setting, the Gothic cathedral became a place of great social interaction and education. For instance, a famous tympanum of *Chartres Cathedral shows Mary as the patroness of the seven *liberal arts.

Gradual. A *responsive *antiphon recited following the first *lesson of the *Liturgy of the Word. It is likely of ancient derivation, the text often taken from the *Psalter. The term derives from Latin *gradus*, a "step" or "walk," that is, the place from which the text was read. *See also* responsorial psalm.

Great Litany. A lengthy, special *litany of the AC for use in various services.

Great Thanksgiving. The *prayer of consecration in the *Liturgy of the Eucharist.

Greco-Russian Rite. The *rite of the Greek and Russian Orthodox family of churches. *See* Byzantine Rite.

Greek. The original language of the NT (specifically *koinē*, "common" Greek) and of much of the ancient church in general (even the early Roman church).

greeting. *See* salutation.

Gregorian calendar. The calendar established in the sixteenth century under Pope Gregory XIII and recognized by the WC. Its gradual deviation over time from the earlier Julian calendar means that the WC and EC usually celebrate *Easter on a different calendar day, as the EC still establishes the date of Easter Sunday according to the Julian calendar.

Gregorian chant. A form of *plainsong whose standardization is attributed to the direction of *Gregory the Great.

Gregory the Great (c. 540-604). The historically significant Roman pope who, among other things, oversaw regulation of church clergy and worship in the WC.

H

Hagia Sophia. Greek for "Holy Wisdom," the great Byzantine *church building in Constantinople (present-day Istanbul). Commissioned by emperor Justinian and dedicated in 537, its central *dome, supported by pendentives, is one of the largest in the world.

Hammond, Peter (1921-1999). An *Anglican *priest who advocated merging modern design for *church buildings with a high regard for patristic liturgical theology (*see* ancient-future). His major work was *Liturgy and Architecture* (1961), where he favored a *Eucharist-oriented functionality in church design (a *domus ecclesiae*) for a service involving both *clergy and *laity that overcomes the medieval tendency to relegate congregants to the role of spectators, a church which thereby becomes a theological symbol (a *domus Dei*).

Handel, George Frideric (1685-1759). A German composer who came to dominate British classical music for well over a hundred years. Recognized as one of the great Baroque composers, he wrote a number of works for sacred texts and biblical themes, his most famous being the *oratorio *Messiah*, whose "Hallelujah" chorus may be the most well-known piece of classical music in the world.

hands, raising of. A *gesture of prayer and adoration (1 Tim 2:8). *See also* orans.

healing service. A special service or *rite in which prayers for the sick are offered. It is founded on the instruction given in James 5:14-15, which prescribes *anointing of the sick. In the history of the RC the rite of anointing the sick was overshadowed by, and applied especially to, the special case of the dying ("extreme unction"), but the two situations are now distinguished. The World Day of the Sick (February 11) was established by Pope John Paul II.

heavenly liturgy. The view that the earthly liturgy reflects or participates in the heavenly worship (Germ. 1; 6), likely as old as the book of Revelation, the Gospel of Matthew (the Lord's Prayer: "on earth as it is in heaven") and Hebrews (Heb 12:22-23). Biblical language implies heavenly access through the liturgy in light of Christ's finished work (Heb 4:14; 7:26; 9:8, 23-24; 10:19, 20). Indeed, Christ the sacrificial Lamb is the center of the heavenly liturgy (Rev 5). In Christian liturgy the *Gloria in Excelsis Deo and the *Sanctus recognize the angelic presence and accompaniment in the service (cf. CCC 1090, 1137, 1326; SC 8). As the temple was the location of the meeting of heaven and earth (cf. Bethel at Gen 28:12, 16-22; 1 Kings 8:27-30; cf. also Gen 11:4), so in the Christian church service the gap between heaven and earth is bridged, especially at the *Communion *table.

Helena, St. (c. 255-c. 330). The mother of Constantine the Great, she was instrumental in the construction of important *church buildings. The *Church of the Holy Sepulchre owes its existence to her impetus.

hero cult. In the Greco-Roman world the powerful dead who in life had contended and suffered with endurance. The tombs of heroes were sacred places, and at their tombs or other shrines dedicated to them people enjoyed annual feasts on the anniversary of their deaths, along with singing of their deeds (e.g., epic poetry) and holding celebratory competitions. Heroes in turn were understood as protectors. They were also frequently associated with the earth's fecundity (Hesiod, *Works and Days* 126, where they are called *ploutodotai*, from Gk. *ploutos*, "wealth"; cf. 2 Kings 13:20-21), an aspect reminiscent of suffering/dying fertility deities (e.g., Attis, Heracles-Melqart). Later Christian veneration of *saints appears to have had some root in hero cults.

The language of the suffering hero is applied to Jesus (Mk 8:31; Heb 5:8; 12:1-3) as well as to Peter and Paul (*1 Clem.* 5; cf. Phil 2:16-17), Polycarp (*Mart. Pol.* 18), and other Christians who contended and suffered for their faith (*1 Clem.* 6; 7). As part of his defense of the Christian faith, Justin Martyr favorably compared Jesus to the Greco-Roman heroes (*1 Apol.* 21; 22; 54; see Riley).

Hildegard of Bingen (1098-1179). A *nun in the Benedictine order. Hildegard was a polymath who, among other things, wrote sacred music.

Hingham Meetinghouse. A Puritan *church building in Hingham, Massachusetts. Built in 1681 and still standing, it exemplifies architecture accommodating the austere *sermon-oriented Puritan service.

Hippolytus (fl. early third century). A Christian martyr who was a teacher and *priest at Rome and to whom many early written works are attributed. The important liturgical work *Apostolic Tradition* is attributed to him, though some scholars doubt this attribution.

holy. Set apart for the deity (Heb. *qōdeš*; Gk. *hagios*; Lat. *sanctus*); separate from the mundane; sacred; pure. *Holy* applies to the place of worship (in Gk. the temple is a *hagion*; *see* sanctuary) and to the objects of the worship service (cf. the Ark of the Covenant at 1 Sam 6:19-20; 2 Sam 6:6, 7). God is holy (Is 6:1-4; 57:15), a consuming, and thus purifying, fire (Heb 12:29), and is to be worshiped with awe and *reverence (cf. Jesus cleansing the temple).

Holy Cross Day (September 14). The day commemorating the dedication of the *Church of the Holy Sepulchre in 335. Color: red.

holy day. A day on which a religious person or event is commemorated, from which the English word *holiday* is derived.

Holy Name of Jesus, Feast of the. A feast rooted in the Middle

Ages, having variable dates: January 1 (*EBCP*); January 2, or Sunday between January 1 and 6 (RC); August 7 (*ABCP*).

Holy Saturday. The day before *Easter, solemnly recognizing Christ in the tomb (i.e., descent into Hades [the place of the dead]). Typically this day enjoys little liturgical celebration until the beginning of the Easter *Vigil Saturday night. Color: white.

Holy Spirit, The. The third person of the Holy *Trinity. Associated with (re)creation and (re)birth (Gen 1:2; Jn 3:5-6; 1 Pet 3:18), the Holy Spirit is a gift to the Christian (Acts 2:38; 10:45) and the Christian community (1 Cor 12:13), not only working in lives but in worship (Jn 4:23; Rom 8:15-16, 26; Gal 4:6; Eph 2:18; 4:3; Phil 3:3; 1 Cor 12:7; Jude 1:20).

Holy Week. The week before *Easter commemorating the *Passion of Jesus Christ. It begins with *Palm Sunday and concludes with *Holy Saturday. The week traces the final events of Jesus' life as given in the *Gospel narratives (generally, Mt 21–28; Mk 11–16; Lk 19–24; Jn 12–20). In the *Didascalia Apostolorum* the six days preceding Easter were considered a *fast. Color: red.

homiletics. The art of *preaching.

homily. Greek *homilia*, "instruction," in a worship service a short *sermon, commentary or exegesis.

horarium. A set pattern of reading the Hours (Lat. *hora*, "hour"). *See* Daily Office.

Horologion. A *liturgical book of the EC for the Hours (Gk. *hōra*, "hour"). *See* Daily Office.

Host. From Latin *hostia*, "sacrificial victim," an RC term for the *consecrated *bread of the *Eucharist.

Hours, Liturgy of the. *See* Daily Office.

hymn. From Greek *hymnos*, a song sung to a deity. The field covering the study and practice of church music is called hymnody. The *Psalter contains many hymns, and Christians sang these (Eph 5:19; Col 3:16; 1 Cor 14:26) and other compositions (Phil 2:6-11; 1 Tim 3:16), and early on new compositions were welcome (Tert., *Apol.* 39). Throughout the Middle Ages hymns, mostly the Psalter, were sung by clerical *choirs, and not by the *laity (in much of the OC singing is done by the *clergy and choir). Modern congregational hymn singing, including newer compositions, essentially began with *Luther, though the Calvinist churches tended toward psalm singing. Later *Watts composed original hymns sung to the older *meters developed for the psalms. *Wesley was influenced by the personal emphasis of the pietists (see Routley). The nineteenth century saw the recapturing of the medieval Latin hymns, this time for congregational singing. Many of the well-known English-language hymns sung in churches today are rooted in the later evangelical movements (*see* gospel song). Revival and evangelistic-meeting songs include "How Great Thou Art!" and "It Is Well with My Soul." A number of women have written hymns, among them Frances Havergal, Christina Rossetti and Fanny *Crosby.

hymn tune. The music to which a *hymn is sung. It is not uncommon for a number of hymns to share the same tune or, on the other hand, for a particular hymn's lyrics to be set to more than one tune. Often the hymn tune carries a name different from the hymn title. *Hymnals distinguish between hymn tunes and their composers, and hymn texts and their hymnists.

hymnal. A book containing *hymns and sometimes other texts for worship. In the English tradition a landmark hymnal is the *English Hymnal* (compiled 1906 by Ralph Vaughan-Williams and Percy Dearmer).

I

I H S. The Latin abbreviation for *Iesus Hominum Salvator*, "Jesus, Savior of Humanity," or a monogram for the Greek form of the name *Jesus* (*Iēsous*).

icon. An image (Gk. *eikōn*, "image," "statue"). In Christian contexts, an image of Jesus or any of the saints is understood as an impulse to, or example of, holiness and faith. An icon is also a window, or a means of access, to the deity or saint who dwells beyond. Many Protestants reject the presence of icons in worship (based on Ex 20:4-6).

Iconoclastic Controversy (726-843). A period in Byzantine church history when the use of *icons was severely debated and even at times officially condemned.

iconography. The practice and study of religious visual imagery.

iconostasis. In the OC a broad screen having three doors that forms a partition between the *nave and the *sanctuary. The name derives from the *icons featured on it (e.g., Jesus, Mary, apostles and angels). The WC *chancel screen (*rood screen*) is analogous.

Incarnation, Feast of the. *See* Annunciation, Feast of the.

incense. A visual and scented *symbol of prayers rising to God (Ps 141:2; Rev 5:8), as well as a symbol of the Holy Spirit (Germ. 30). Incense dispersed over the *altar also represents the spices brought by the women for the embalmment of Jesus. Burning incense is often contained in a *censer.

inclusive language. The use of liturgical language that does not discriminate some congregants from others (based on, e.g., gender, ethnicity; cf. Gal 3:28).

inculturation. Regarding liturgy, the dynamic process whereby liturgical traditions developed within one culture are assimilated and adapted by another culture having its own established religio-cultural beliefs and practices (e.g., as occurs in crosscultural mission work). Inculturation has been an ongoing process within the history of Christianity. *See also Our Modern Services.*

Independence Day (July 4). The day American independence was declared (1776), observed in the calendar of the *EBCP* as well as by many other churches in the U.S.

infant baptism. *See* baptism, infant.

Initiation. *See* baptism.

Innocents, Day of Holy (December 28). The commemoration of the children murdered by Herod the Great (Mt 2:13-18).

intercession. A form of *prayer in which requests are made for, or on behalf of, others (1 Tim 2:1-4). Always a part of corporate worship, prayer on behalf of others is the function of the priesthood of all believers (see Bradshaw [B]). *Intercessions* also refers to the intercessory prayer that takes place during the *Liturgy of the Eucharist.

introit. An introductory *psalm or other Scripture (from Lat. *introitus*, "entrance"). It may open the service or open the *Liturgy of the Word after *confession and *absolution. Sometimes it is followed by an *antiphon ("Entrance Antiphon") and then usually by the *Gloria Patri.

invitation. In the *revival service of worship, the offer of salvation in Christ to the unconverted; the call for a *decision to choose Christ. At times perceived as the ultimate goal of the service, it usually comes at the end and may be associated with an *altar call.

Invitatory. The opening section of the *Daily Office just before the *psalmody. Typical *Morning Prayer Invitatory begins with "Lord, open our lips / And our mouth shall proclaim your praise" (Ps 51:15; Ps 19:14 is also used), *Gloria Patri, and then the invitatory psalm, usually the *Venite or *Jubilate, along with an *antiphon. *Evening Prayer may open with "O God, make speed to save us / O Lord, make haste to help us," Gloria Patri and, optionally, an invitatory psalm. Other invitatory psalms include 100, 67 and 24.

invocation. A prayer inviting the presence of the deity (i.e., the Holy *Trinity) at the beginning of the service. The *epiclesis is also an invocation said during the *Anaphora.

Iona Community (founded 1938). An ecumenical Christian community on the historic island of Iona off the coast of Scotland. Made up of both *clergy and *laity, the community, among other things, develops and publishes materials for Christian worship.

isometric. Literally "equal measure," church music that has an even, steady quality, in other words, less rhythmic in structure.

ΙΧΘΥΣ. The *Greek word for *"fish," an ancient Christian *confessional acrostic for *Jesus*: Ι = Jesus (*Iēsous*); Χ = Christ (*Christos*); ΘΥ = God's Son (*Theou Huios*); Σ = Savior (*Sōtēr*).

J

James, Feast of Apostle (July 25). The day commemorating the fisherman James "the Great" who, along with his younger brother the apostle John, was a son of Zebedee (Mt 4:21), both sons designated "Sons of Thunder" by Jesus (Mk 3:17). James was one of the first of the Twelve to suffer martyrdom (Acts 12:2), though legend has him previously accomplishing missionary work in Spain, of which he is the patron saint. The church at *Santiago de Compostela was one of the most celebrated pilgrimage destinations in the Middle Ages. The EC celebrates his day on April 30.

James the Just, Feast of (October 23). The day commemorating the brother (or cousin) of Jesus. James became the well-known leader of the church at Jerusalem (Acts 21:17-18) and is considered its first *bishop. His apostleship is unclear, though there are grounds for it (Gal 1:19). The NT epistle of James is credited to him. The ancient liturgy bearing his name is much later in date and contains the famous *Cherubic *Hymn, "Let All Mortal Flesh Keep Silent."

Jesus Christ. The Son of God incarnate, the second person of the Holy *Trinity, and thus to be worshiped (Jn 20:28; Phil 2:5-11; Rev 5:12). He is the ground of all Christian *worship (Jn 10:9; 14:6; cf. Mt 11:27), both as the cause (Rom 5:1; Eph 2:18; Heb 3:1, 6; 6:20; 9:11-15; 10:19-22) and as continuing mediator (1 Tim 2:5; Heb 7:25; 13:15), and through the *Eucharist he sustains his church. The *liturgical year revolves around his life given in the *Gospels, and the weekly Sunday feast celebrates his resurrection. The title *Christos* is the Greek equivalent of Hebrew *māšīāḥ*, "Messiah," or "anointed one." *See also* ΙΧΘΥΣ.

Jesus (iconography). Pictorial representations of Jesus that have varied over time, though predominantly focusing on his birth, death and exaltation. However, in the most ancient Christian art, he is portrayed as young, beardless and actively working miracles, as well as at times represented within a traditionally pagan form, such as Orpheus or the *Good Shepherd. In post-Constantinian art he is bearded and often represented as the *Pantocrator. This representation of Jesus as cosmic ruler and judge continues throughout history, though in the WC there is also an emphasis on his suffering and death (e.g., crucifixion and Pietà). Additionally, the Madonna and child motif, found as early as the *catacombs, enjoys continuous representation both in the EC and the WC. Modern representations of Jesus include depictions of his ministry as found in the *Gospels. A popular modern representation is *Head of Christ* by Warner Sallman (1941).

John the Baptist, Nativity of (June 24). A major observance remembering the birth of this prophetic precursor of Jesus Christ (Mk 1:2-9 par.). He is prominent in medieval art, usually flanking Jesus (along with the Virgin *Mary).

Jonah. The OT prophet whose story about being swallowed by a sea creature and then regurgitated onto land (Jon 1–2) was noted by Jesus as a type of his own death, burial and resurrection (Mt 12:40). The story of Jonah and the sea creature was a popular motif in Christian funerary art (*see* catacombs, Christian Roman).

Jubilate. Latin for "Make a joyful noise," the first word of Psalm 100. Traditionally assigned to *Morning Prayer.

Judica. Psalm 43 (42), traditionally said at the beginning of the WC service for the fifth *Sunday of *Lent.

K

kephalaia. A *Greek term meaning "chapters," the paragraph (*lection) divisions found in a number of ancient Greek manuscripts of the NT.

King James Version. *See* Authorized Version.

Kiss of Peace. A part of the eucharistic *rite (Cyr., *Myst. Cat.* 5.3) as early as Justin Martyr (*1 Apol.* 65; also Tert., *Or.* 18) and emphasizing reconciliation and *unity. There are many NT precedents (Rom 16:16; 1 Cor 16:20; 2 Cor 13:12; 1 Thess 5:26; 1 Pet 5:14). The ritual is still recognized in the *Coptic Church, and a *peace (*Pax Domini*) is part of some WC eucharistic liturgies.

kneeling. A *gesture of humility and supplication (Mt 17:14; 20:20). *Genuflexion* is touching one knee to the ground.

koinonia. A *Greek term meaning "holding in common" or "fellowship," an early mark of Christian gatherings (Acts 2:42). The English term *communion* is based on *koinōnia*, the *Eucharist being a "participation in" the blood and body of Jesus (1 Cor 10:16; for baptism cf. Cyr., *Myst. Cat.* 2.7).

Kyrie Eleison. *Greek for "Lord have mercy," a *supplication that is the part of the *Ordinary of the Latin *Mass (cf. Mk 10:47).

Kyrie Pantocrator. Greek for "Lord Almighty," a short book of the *Apocrypha, also titled *The Prayer of Manasseh*, used by Christians as a *canticle.

L

labyrinth. A maze-like pattern on the *nave floors of a number of medieval *Gothic cathedrals dedicated to the Virgin *Mary (e.g., *Chartres Cathedral), as well as some other churches. The design form is quite ancient, long predating Christianity and perhaps associated with goddess cult. Its reemergence in the High Middle Ages is not clearly understood but does coincide with the rise of the *cult of the Virgin.

Lamb of God. A designation of Jesus in the Gospel of John (Jn 1:29,

36), and a visual *symbol of Jesus that emerged in Christian *iconography. *See also* Agnus Dei; Paschal Lamb.

Last Supper. In the Synoptic *Gospels, the final meal Jesus had with his disciples before his *Passion, a meal in which Jesus established the Christian *sacrament of the *Eucharist. All three Synoptics have the meal take place at the time of the *Passover, and thus it is a Passover meal (Mt 26:17-19 par.). The Gospel of John, however, appears to place the final gathering of Jesus and his disciples the day before Passover (Jn 13:1-2), though the chronology in John is not quite clear. At any rate, though it notes the betrayal of Jesus, the supper narrative in the Gospel of John does not contain the institution of the Eucharist. Instead, John tells of Jesus' washing the disciples' feet (*see* foot washing), having already earlier given his eucharistic theology (Jn 6:47-58). The Last Supper has been the subject of major paintings by Leonardo da Vinci (1495-1498) and Salvador Dalí (1955).

Latin. The language of the ancient Romans and official language of the RC.

Lauds. A morning *office named after the praise ("Hallel") psalms (148–150; Lat. *laudes*), in which they were sung, perhaps rooted in the liturgical practice of the synagogue. In the AC *Cranmer combined elements of *Matins and Lauds to form *Morning Prayer.

Law, reading of the. Readings from the Law of Moses, in particular the *Decalogue. This practice is traditional in many churches, such as in preparation for corporate *confession of sin. Sometimes a reading of the Law precedes the *Eucharist, such reading being a preparation for approaching the *Table of the Lord, which is a table of grace.

lay, laity. Derived from Greek *laos*, "people" (e.g., Mt 1:21; 2:6), those not officially part of the *clergy or *religious.

laying on of hands. An act of authoritative *consecration (Acts 6:6; 13:3), especially with baptism (cf. Acts 8:17), but sometimes associated with *healing (Acts 9:12; cf. 9:17 where all three aspects are present) as well as *ordination. *See also* confirmation.

Lazarus. The man Jesus raised from the dead in John 11:1-53. In *catacomb art he is represented as a smaller person wrapped in funerary dressings, Jesus attending with a *rhabdos* (wand).

Lazarus Saturday. The Saturday preceding *Palm Sunday. In the

Gospel of John the *pericope concerning the raising of Lazarus (Jn 11:1-53) immediately precedes the beginning of the *Holy Week narrative, foreshadowing the resurrection of Jesus eight days later.

lectern. A type of *pulpit from which *lessons are given.

lectio continua. The practice of consecutive *reading of a book of the Bible in consecutive liturgical services, whether the Sunday service or the *Daily Office.

lectio selecta. The reading of *lessons appropriate for services on *holy days, *feasts and *fasts.

lection. A term synonymous with *lesson.

lectionary. Book(s) containing the full text of appointed Scripture *lessons for the Christian *calendar (*Sundays and *holy days) and for the *Daily Office. It is unknown when lectionaries began to exist as separate works, but ancient divisions within certain NT manuscripts indicate that lessons were already marked off quite early (see Codex Vaticanus), and lection divisions can be found in the margins of the Nestle-Aland/UBS edition of the Greek NT (see kephalaia).

The term *lectionary* also refers simply to a table of lessons appointed for the *Liturgy of the Word and for the *Daily Office. Generally in the past lectionaries were arranged around a one-year cycle (e.g., the ABCP), assigning to each week a *Gospel lesson and another NT lesson (the Epistles, Acts or Revelation). A three-year Sunday and festal lectionary was developed in the RC (1969, rev. 1981) in response to *Vatican II directives, assigning for each occasion three lessons: generally the OT, the NT (the Epistles from Advent through Easter, and thereafter Acts and Revelation) and a Gospel. Year A revolves around the Gospel of Matthew, B around Mark and C around Luke, with John's Gospel interspersed yearly. The OT lessons (accompanied by an appropriate *psalm) often thematically match the Gospel lessons. This three-year lectionary is approximated in the EBCP. A two-year cycle of lessons was developed in the RC for weekday *Masses, and the EBCP includes a two-year cycle of lessons for the Daily Office.

The *Revised Common Lectionary* (RCL) published in 1992 is a Protestant three-year lectionary (of ecumenical intent) that is somewhat correlated, but not entirely, to the three-year lectionary developed in the RC. After Pentecost the *RCL* differs from the RC lectionary in its OT lessons, emphasizing certain OT sections: Year A, the Heptateuch; B, David, Solomon and the Wisdom books; C, certain prophets. Yet, optional OT lessons more in line with RC and LC preferences are also included. The *RCL* is now acceptable to the Protestant Episcopal Church in the United States of America in lieu of the lectionary in the *EBCP*, and is also followed to some extent in the *Anglican *Common Worship.

legomena. A *Greek term meaning "things that are said." In Greek religion the sacred words spoken in *cult, such as the *hieros logos*, "sacred story," loosely corresponding to the term *mythos*.

Lent, Lenten season. From Middle English *lenten*, "spring," the forty-day period of *fasting and repentance that lasts from *Ash Wednesday into *Holy Week (excepting the six Sundays). These forty days parallel Jesus' great fast (Mt 4:2), which was a struggle with the devil, as well as the forty-year wandering in the wilderness of the children of Israel.

Though the Lenten season is not found in Scripture, from early times Christians have set aside some time before Easter for intensified catechism (i.e., preparation for *baptismal initiation on Easter Sunday). Table 1 shows the Lenten lessons of the Greek Church (from Scrivener).

Table 1. Lenten Lessons of the Greek Church

Saturday		Sunday	
Mk 2:23–3:5	Heb 1:1-12	Jn 1:44-51	Heb 11:24-40
Mk 1:35-44	Heb 3:12-14	Mk 2:1-12	Heb 1:10–2:3
Mk 2:14-17	Heb 10:32-37	Mk 8:34–9:1	Heb 4:14–5:6
Mk 7:31-37	Heb 6:9-12	Mk 9:17-31	Heb 6:13-20
Mk 8:27-31	Heb 9:24-28	Mk 10:32-45	Heb 9:11-14
Jn 11:1-45	Heb 12:28–13:8	(Palm Sunday)	

lesson. From Latin *lectio*, a portion of Scripture read for the liturgy of a particular day; synonymous with *reading*. *See also lectio continua; lectio selecta; lectionary; pericope.*

lex orandi, lex credendi. A Latin expression meaning "the rule of what is prayed is the rule of what is believed," in other words, as one worships, so one believes.

liberal arts, the seven. From Latin *liber*, "free," the arts of the free person, rooted in the classical tradition, that formed the basis of medieval education. The seven liberal arts are comprised of the trivium (grammar, dialectic and rhetoric) and the quadrivium (geometry, arithmetic, astronomy and music). In the Middle Ages *cathedral schools were centers of education and the Virgin *Mary became the patroness of the liberal arts.

Lima Liturgy (1982). An idealized service of worship (including celebration of the *Eucharist) developed by the World Council of Churches and exemplifying the recommendations of *Baptism, Eucharist and Ministry*.

litany. In liturgy a formal series of requests before God (from Gk. *litanos*, "prayerful petitioning"). Often the form of the litany comprises the leader making various *petitions and the people intermittingly responding (e.g., "Have mercy upon us"). Litanies are especially appropriate during times of distress. They are prominent in the Orthodox liturgy, and the *African American Heritage Hymnal* contains numerous litanies.

liturgical book. A book that provides the order and content for the service of worship, such as the *Roman Catholic *Missal*, the *Anglican *Book of Common Prayer*, the Orthodox *Euchologion*, Lutheran *hymnals, the *Presbyterian *Book of Common Order, The United Methodist Book of Worship*, and less binding Protestant service books and minister's manuals.

Some have detected liturgical tendencies in the *Gospels of John and Mark; indeed, liturgical elements are established in the Gospels and emphasized in other parts of the NT, functioning therefore as early liturgical books of the church.

liturgical dance. A dance that takes place as part of the worship service. Precedent can be found in the OT (2 Sam 6:14; Eccles 3:4; Ps 149), and Greco-Roman *cults frequently included dance (e.g., the *orchēstra*, "dancing space," as part of Dionysian tragedy; cults of Isis and Cybele). Yet there are no references in the NT to dancing as part of public worship. Religio-cultural presuppositions tend to influence its incorporation into the modern worship service of the WC.

liturgical drama. A mytho-cultic *religious reenactment of a significant religious story or event (*mythos* understood as *hieros logos*, "sacred story"). Isaiah 40–55 has recently been argued to be an ancient liturgical drama (including hymns, processions and dance; see Baltzer), and Western theater itself is rooted in religious *cult (i.e., that of Dionysus). Traditionally, Christian liturgy has included an element of liturgical drama, especially at the *Eucharist. Indeed, many liturgies are dramas to some extent. An early dramatic reenactment of the women at the Easter tomb was the *Quem quaeritis* (WC, developed early Middle Ages). The term *liturgical drama* is also applied to medieval *mystery plays. *See also drōmena; legomena.*

liturgical movement. The prolonged modern reflection by academics and clergy on the history, meaning and restoration of Christian liturgies (both Protestant and RC). The movement gave particular attention to ancient elements of worship and participation by the *laity (1 Pet 2:5), yet with an eye to modern ideas and concerns. It began somewhat in the nineteenth century and culminated, for example, with the liturgical directives of *Vatican II. *See also* Baumstark, Anton; Dix, Gregory.

liturgical year. The annual cycle of seasons, *holy days, *feasts and *fasts for the Christian church. *Fixed* observances are set according to the dates of the secular calendar, and *movable feasts*, in the main, are set by the astronomically determined date of *Easter. EC calendars may differ from WC in that the former tends to follow the older Julian calendar, the latter the *Gregorian.

Although early Christian *calendars are first recorded in the WC, the Christian liturgical year already had precedent in the Jewish calendar and the one-year ministry of Jesus presented in the *Gospel of Mark. The Jewish people have enjoyed a liturgical year built around the agricultural and moon cycles, a liturgical year for the most part prescribed in the OT. So Christians have done the same, adapting certain Jewish days and developing other days of commemoration reflecting the life and ministry of Jesus. The result is a yearly cycle of reflection on, and celebration of, both redemption in Christ and being Christian in the world, with the creation itself affirmed as the liturgical year intertwines with the cycles of planting and harvest, of the *moon and the sun.

In the EC the Christian year begins on September 1, perhaps drawing a connection with Rosh Hashanah, the beginning of the Jewish civil year. (The Jewish religious year begins in the spring.) In the WC the liturgical year begins on the first *Sunday of *Advent, the date of which is determined by the Feast of St. *Andrew.

Paul takes no aversion to Jewish *holy days (1 Cor 16:8; cf. Acts 20:16), nor the *Sabbath (Rom 14:5), but associates important Christian *rites (*baptism and *Eucharist) with OT themes (1 Cor 10:1-4), so long as it is not a legal obligation (Col 2:16) or so long as astrological biases do not creep in (Gal 4:8-10). Creation, including time, is redeemed in Christ (Col 2:16-17), not negated. The WC liturgical seasons, allowing for variations, are as follows:

Advent	Sunday closest to November 30 through day before Christmas
Christmas	Christmas Day through Baptism of Our Lord *or* Candlemas
Ordinary Time	The following day through the day before Ash Wednesday
Lent	Ash Wednesday through Holy Saturday
Easter	Easter Sunday through Pentecost
Ordinary Time	The following day through the day before the beginning of Advent

liturgy. From Greek *leitourgia*, "religious service" (e.g., Lk 1:23; Phil 2:17; Heb 8:6; 9:21; *1 Clem.* 40.2, 5; 44.2; cf. verb *leitourgeō* at Acts 13:2; Heb 10:11), a corporate religious service rendered to God by the people, including *Sunday worship, the *Daily Office, *baptism, the *Eucharist, etc. The liturgy is a *drama involving both God and the people, the "exchange of prayers and graces" (see Baumstark), taking place in *sacred time and in *sacred space.

Ancient liturgy involved (1) things that are said (Gk. *legomena*; Cyr., *Procatech.* 11, 12), that is, sacred sayings and stories; (2) things that are done (Gk. *drōmena*), that is, ritual actions/*gestures. Both categories are rooted in ancient Greek religion (cf. Pausanias 2.37.2) and applicable to many religions under the expression *myth and ritual.*

Liturgy of the Eucharist. The section of the worship service devoted to *Communion. It follows the *Liturgy of the Word and the *offertory. Order and elements vary somewhat, but generally, especially in the WC, the service of the Eucharist approximates that laid out in table 2.

Table 2. Western Eucharistic Liturgy

Anaphora (made up of the Preface, Eucharistic Prayer and Communion):
    Preface, including the following:
        Preparation and Introductory Dialogue, including Sursum Corda
        Vere dignum: "It is meet and right . . ."
        Preface for the day
        Sanctus
        Benedictus Qui Venit
        Prayer of Humble Access [AC]
    Eucharistic Prayer (prayer of consecration), which includes the following:
        Prayer of thanks to the Father for the gift of the Son
        Words of Institution
        Anamnesis
        Epiclesis
        Intercessions
        Lord's Prayer
        Peace of the Lord (*Pax Domini*)
        Agnus Dei
    Communion, including the breaking of bread and distribution
Nunc Dimittis
Post-Communion prayer of thanksgiving and blessing
Dismissal

The earliest nonbiblical eucharistic order is given in *Didache* 9-10, making reference to Jesus as "the child" (Gk. *pais*; cf. *Ap. Trad.* 4.4, 13), and Christ's body and blood referenced through symbolic language ("holy vine" and bread "fragments"). In the second century Justin Martyr's Eucharist (*1 Apol.* 65) included the *prayers, the *kiss of peace, presentation of gifts of *bread, *wine and *water, the *thanksgiving (Creator, Son and Holy Spirit), the assent of the people, and distribution by the deacons (cf. Acts 6). The order is not far off from that of the *Eucharist of the *Apostolic Tradition* (chap. 4). Comparison should also be made to that of Cyril of Jerusalem (*Myst. Cat.* 5): (1) *ablution; (2) kiss of peace; (3) *Sursum Corda; (4) thanksgiving; (5) allusion to Psalm 34:3; (6) *Sanctus; (7) *Epiclesis; (8) *intercessions; (9) the *Lord's Prayer; (10) Psalm 34:8 ("O taste and see"); and (11) Communion (lacking the *Words of Institution). The *Liturgy of St. Mark* (late fifth century, Egypt) also contains most of the above.

Liturgy of the Word. The section of the worship service that focuses on *lessons from the Scriptures. Always preceding the *Liturgy of the Eucharist (as early as Justin, *1 Apol.* 67), it usually includes the *homily/*sermon and *intercessions (cf. CCC 1349). The WC form approximates what is found in table 3.

Table 3. Liturgy of the Word (WC)

First lesson (OT, if included)
Responsorial Psalm or Gradual
Second lesson (Epistle)
Response, *Alleluia* or Gloria Patri
Gospel lesson
Creed
Homily/sermon
Hymn of response
Intercessions/prayers of the people
Exchanges of peace

Lord's Day, the. *Sunday, celebrated as the day Jesus rose from the dead (Mt 28:1 par.). The expression itself is found at Revelation 1:10. This "first day of the week" became the primary day of Christian corporate worship (Acts 20:7; Jn 20:19, 26; 1 Cor 16:2; Justin, *1 Apol.* 67).

Lord's Prayer, the. Also called the Our Father (Lat. *Pater Noster*), a part of Christian liturgy at least as early as the *Didache*, which instructs recitation three times a day (*Did.* 8.2-3). It is the *prayer that Jesus taught his disciples to pray (Mt 6:9-13; Lk 11:2-4), both as one prescribed (Lk 11:2) and as an example (Mt 6:9). It is divided into an opening address, seven *petitions and a *doxology.

Along with the *Apostles' Creed it was part of ancient catechetical instruction (Cyr., *Myst. Cat.* 5) and likewise not to be recited
in front of outsiders (see Kelly). It is traditionally part of the *eucharistic service, being recited either before or after the *Communion (though in P&RC it may appear before the *confession and
*absolution). Indeed, a eucharistic interpretation of the Prayer is
not without precedent, the "daily bread" being equated to the eucharistic bread (Cyr., *Myst. Cat.* 5.15), recalling the daily provision
of manna from heaven (Ex 16:4; cf. Jn 6:32).

There are parallels between the Lord's Prayer and the eucharistic liturgy of *Didache* 9-10. The Lord's Prayer includes *epi-
cletic language referencing the name of the deity and invoking
the manifestation of God's heavenly rule on earth, as well as the
prayer for "daily bread." The eucharistic prayer of thanksgiving
in the *Didache* contains the ancient prayer "Maranatha" (*Did.* 10.6:
Aram. *Our Lord, come!;* cf. 1 Cor 16:22; Rev 22:17, 20; CCC 1130), the
text also mentioning the "holy name" (*Did.* 10.2). The doxologies
at *Didache* 10.2, 4, reflect the ending added to the Lord's Prayer in
later manuscripts of Matthew's Gospel (6:13: *yours . . . is the glory
forever;* cf. also *Did.* 9.2), and the petition to be delivered from evil
is also present in both prayers (Mt 6:13; *Did.* 10.5).

Exegesis of the Prayer is typical of the *catechetical tradition
(e.g., Cyr., *Myst. Cat.* 5.11-18; CCC 2759-865; cf. Tert., *Or.* 1-10), a tradition retained by the Reformers (e.g., *Luther's Sm. Cat. 3; Heid.
Cat. 119-29; cf. *West. Short. Cat.* 98-107).

Lord's Supper. *See* Eucharist.

Lord's Table. *See* Eucharist.

Love Feast. (1) The *Agape; (2) the communal meal that arose
among certain RR groups and spread to those influenced by them
(e.g., Methodists). This agape meal is often associated with *Communion and, among certain groups, with *foot washing, and the
term *Love Feast* frequently is the general name for the *ordinance
that includes all three components.

Lucernarium. *See* service of light.

Lucia, Feast of St. (December 13). A feast in honor of an early
fourth-century martyr, whose date of commemoration was once
connected with the old Julian calendar occurrence of the winter
*solstice (cf. the title of John Donne's poem "A Nocturnal upon S.

Lucy's Day, Being the Shortest Day"). According to today's calendar, December 13 in the northerly latitudes is the approximate time in the year when the sun ceases to set at a time earlier than the day before and looks forward to the sun setting later. Therefore the date of the feast is appropriate for a saint with "light" in her name. Festivals of light have traditionally been associated with her, for example, the popular Scandinavian festivals. She is the patron saint of the blind. Color: white.

Luther, Martin (1483-1546). A German theologian, reformer and Bible translator, originally an Augustinian *monk. Luther was a liturgical reformer (*Deutsche Messe*, 1526) who believed that what did not contradict the gospel could be retained in the liturgy. Also an important *hymn writer (e.g., "A Mighty Fortress Is Our God"), he is often credited with beginning the Protestant Reformation when he nailed his *Ninety-five Theses* to the Wittenberg church door (October 31, 1517; *see* Reformation Day).

Lutheran hymnal. A *liturgical book of the LC which contains, along with the *hymns, various liturgies for *Sunday worship, the *Daily Office and *baptism (among other things).

lxx. Abbreviation for the *Septuagint.

M

Magna et Mirabilia. Latin for "great and amazing," the song of the martyrs in the book of *Revelation (Rev 15:3-4).

Magnificat. The song the Virgin *Mary sings when visiting her relative Elizabeth (Lk 1:46-55), the first line being, "My soul magnifies [Lat. *magnificat*] the Lord." The song is one of three *canticles in the first two chapters of the Gospel of Luke and is appropriate at *Evening Prayer (cf. prayer of Hannah, 1 Sam 2:1-10).

Marriage rite. The order of worship for a wedding. In the OC and RC, marriage is one of seven *sacraments, and thus ecclesiastical sanction is mandatory. Most Protestant churches do not recognize marriage as a sacrament but rather a civil act having divine *blessing, which is often solemnized with wedding services in churches. The most familiar text for a wedding ceremony within English-speaking Protestantism is that of the Anglican Church, found in the *ABCP*.

Mary, the Virgin. The *virgin (Gk. *parthenos*) mother of Jesus Christ (Mt 1:23; Lk 1:27; Ign., *Smyrn.* 1; *Eph.* 19.1). Designated *Theotokos* (Gk. for *God-bearer*, interpreted by some as *Mother of God*) at the Council of Ephesus (431), the title is recognized not only by the OC and RC, but by a number of Protestants as well. The title is at least as early as the third century in Egypt (in the prayer known as the *Sub tuum praesidium*). Her importance was manifest by the early second century (Ign., *Eph.* 7.2; 19.1), and if the Beloved Disciple of the Gospel of John can be taken as a stand-in for all Christians, she then enjoys an elevated position quite early (Jn 19:26-27). She is understood both as a figure of the church (Rev 12:1-6) and the New Eve (Iren., *Haer.* 3.22.4; CCC 511), as well as associated in ancient Christianity with the life-giving work of the Holy Spirit (e.g., *Apostles' Creed; Iren., *Haer.* 4.33.11).

Mary's virginity not only emphasizes her purity, but also that the child conceived is the Son of God, a concept quite familiar to the earliest Christians as certain pagan heroes were also the off-spring of a virgin and a deity (e.g., Heracles, Asclepius, Perseus; cf. Justin, *1 Apol.* 21-2, 54, where such analogy is part of a *defense* of the Christian faith). The virgin birth therefore has meaning beyond only biological wonder or concerns about original sin.

Many *feast days are associated with Mary, often originating in the EC. Her primary feast day is The Assumption of Mary (August 15). Her Nativity is celebrated September 8 (e.g., *ABCP*, OC) or January 1 (RC). The *Annunciation is March 25, and the Visitation with Elizabeth (Lk 1:39-56) is celebrated May 31 (established thirteenth century; originally July 2, the date the AC now recognizes; *see also* Magnificat). Her Purification is remembered on February 1 or 2 (*see* Candlemas), and her association with the Life-Giving Spring is recognized in the EC on Bright Friday following *Easter. The Immaculate Conception (i.e., born without original sin) is celebrated December 8 (WC origin). In the Americas she is also celebrated as Our Lady of Guadalupe (feast day December 12).

Christianity did not eliminate the imagery of the divine feminine but retained it in the person of the Theotokos (Rev 12:1; CCC 507; cf. the ancient Christian hymn *Ave Stella Maris*), and also in the church itself (*see* font, baptismal). The feminine aspect of the life-giving Spirit was also maintained within certain Gnostic traditions (Iren., *Haer.* 1.5.6; 1.7.2; 1.30.1; Hippolytus, *Refutation of All Heresies* 5.3). *See also* dove; Epiphany, Feast of the.

Mass. Another name for the *Eucharist. As the Eucharist, the Mass has always been the chief religious celebration of Christian churches. Imbedded within the term *Mass* is the intention of preparing the congregation to go out into the world (from Lat. *Missa*, derived from *mitto*, "to send," i.e., *dismissal*, and thus also *mission*). The specific term *Mass* has generally been avoided by many Protestants due to reticence concerning "the sacrifice of the Mass" of the RC liturgy, though parts of the Mass may be retained in Protestant worship (e.g., the *Kyrie Eleison).

Masses can be distinguished between High Mass, which is sung, and Low Mass, which is typically spoken. The Mass sung as a *concert performance* is traditionally divided into five *Ordinary sections that the congregation traditionally sings: (1) Kyrie Eleison, (2) *Gloria in Excelsis Deo, (3) *Credo, (4) *Sanctus, (5) *Agnus Dei. Any of these five sections may be further divided into more complex musical settings. Among the most famous musical settings of the Mass are *Bach's Mass in B minor and Beethoven's Mass in D major (*Missa Solemnis*).

Matins (Mattins). Historically, the early-morning, *vigil-like *monastic *office (cf. Fr. *matin*, "morning"). The term is retained for *Morning Prayer in the AC.

Maundy Thursday. The Thursday of *Holy Week, a major *holy day recognized since the fourth century. On this day Jesus washed his disciples' feet (Jn 13:4-5) and gave the new commandment (Lat. *mandatum*) to love one another (Jn 13:34). The Synoptic Gospels have the *Last Supper occurring on this day, and thus the *Eucharist is celebrated on Maundy Thursday in many churches. Color: red, but white if the Eucharist is celebrated.

means of grace. The means by which the Holy Spirit communicates salvation and sanctification to believers, namely the *Word of God and, in many traditions, the *sacraments (see Aug. Conf. 13; Heid. Cat. 65; CCC 1127).

Melito of Sardis. The Syrian author of *Peri Pascha* (written c. 170), an ancient liturgical *homily for *Easter.

meter. In church hymnody the pattern of syllables of a particular *hymn text, which takes into account the number of syllables per line. The meter is designated by numbers indicating syllables per line (e.g., *Watts's "Our God, Our Help in Ages Past" has the meter 8.6.8.6). A hymn text is sung to a *hymn tune that can accommodate the text's particular meter.

metrical psalms. Psalm texts set to specific *meters. Some churches, especially within the P&RC, sing the *psalms (sometimes *a cappella) to *hymn tunes that accommodate the meters of the psalms.

Midnight Mass. The religious service on *Christmas Eve near the midnight hour. Originating in nineteenth-century England, with impetus in the twentieth century from King's College, Cambridge University, many churches now offer a service of *lessons and *carols on Christmas Eve.

midweek service. A less formal religious gathering, part of the Protestant legacy (e.g., Puritans, Methodists) since at least *Calvin. In the U.S. Wednesday night is often the midweek opportunity for the congregation to meet and encourage each other in the Word, *prayer and testimony.

minister. A person who performs the work of the liturgy with and on behalf of the congregation. In some churches the presiding minister also participates on behalf of Christ (*see* priest).

Missal. A book containing the *order of worship, *rubrics, *prayers and Scripture *lessons for the RC *Mass (Lat. *Missa*).

mode. From Latin *modus,* "manner," a specific musical scale (of tones and semitones). Each particular mode is known by the standardized intervals of the notes of the scale, intervals which vary from mode to mode. Church music traditionally uses the diatonic scale of seven notes, of which eight different modes were employed during the Middle Ages, their names and enumeration as follows: Dorian (I), Phrygian (III), Lydian (V), Mixolydian (VII), with Hypodorian (II) and so forth. Since the seventeenth century, Western music tends to be composed in the Aeolian (IX, the modern minor) and Ionian (XI, the modern major) modes/scales, which is one reason why ancient chants or hymns can seem strange to modern ears.

These modes were named by the ancient Greeks originally after seven Greek tribes. The seven notes of the scales were analogous to the seven planets known in antiquity (and thus the Pythagorean notion of the "music of the spheres"), a relationship implied in the Roman Pantheon.

monastery. A religious complex for the *regular *clergy. A monastery (Gk. *monastērion,* "minster") includes at least a *church building and residences for the *monks, though many monasteries are quite extensive and include, for example, gardens and work areas. The function of the monastery is to designate a self-sustaining place separate from the rest of the world. *See also* abbey; abbot; monk.

monasticism. The *ascetic life of living in a *monastery.

monk. From Greek *monachos,* "solitary," a *clerical or *religious person who takes *vows and isolates himself from the world through *monasticism or some other form of *ascetic existence.

moon, month. Both terms derived from the same Proto-Indo-European root, as the cycle of the moon is about the length of a month. The lunar cycle in the OT begins with the *new moon* (Heb. *ḥōdeš*), which is when the moon is invisible or barely visible as a slim waxing crescent, and this is the beginning of a *month.* The *full moon* occurs about fourteen days, or halfway, into the cycle. This cycle is critical to determining Jewish feasts (Ps 81:3; Hos 2:11), as well as Christian *Easter.

In antiquity, the moon holds a special place as symbolic of the recurring cycle of feminine fertility. The relationship is as ancient as the Gravettian culture in France, where a rock carving shows a pregnant female figure holding a crescent moon or horn with 13 marks (a solar year of 365 ¼ days yields between 12 and 13 moon cycles). With its waxing and waning, the moon also symbolizes growth and decline, as well as the cycle of birth, death and rebirth.

morality play. A medieval Christian *drama centered around personal character, with virtues and vices personified. These plays were separate from the liturgy, organized by the *laity rather than the *clergy and performed outside the *church building. *See also* mystery plays.

Morning Prayer. A part of the *Daily Office, called *Matins in the AC, *Lauds in the RC and Orthros in the *Byzantine Rite. Christians originally may have been influenced by Jewish custom (e.g., Ps 3 and 5 are morning prayers). Morning Prayer spiritually follows the natural rhythm of the day as every morning is a reminder of the resurrection of Jesus (*1 Clem.* 24.1-3), and thus one faced *east during Morning Prayer in late antiquity. Traditional recitations for Morning Prayer include the *Venite and *Jubilate and the *canticles *Te Deum and *Benedictus (and on *Sundays, Dan 3:52-90 LXX). In the twentieth century the Sunday worship services of some churches within the *Wesleyan tradition have been influenced by *Anglican Morning Prayer, as Morning Prayer was often the first part of non-eucharistic Sunday morning services in the Anglican Church (an order of Matins-*Great Litany-*Antecommunion).

motet. Originally a polyphonic musical form for voices (sung *a cappella) that developed during the Middle Ages. As a religious form, it paralleled the secular *madrigal*.

movable feasts. *Holy days whose observance varies on the *calendar from year to year. Most of their dates are determined by the date of *Easter for any particular year.

music. An essential part of Christian worship, prescribed in the NT (Eph 5:19; Col 3:16: "psalms, hymns, and spiritual songs"), much as music was part of OT worship (Ps 134; 135; 2 Chron 7:6; Ezra 3:11), exemplified in the Song of Moses (Ex 15:1-18), the Song of Miriam (Ex 15:21), the Song of Deborah (Judg 5) and David's Song (2 Sam 22; Ps 18). *See also* a cappella; chant; hymn; praise.

mystagogy. A post-baptismal instruction given initiates to explain the ritual(s) they have undergone, the most famous of which is that of Cyril of Jerusalem. *See also deiknymena*.

mystery. Something sacred (e.g., knowledge, story, event or action) that, previously secret or hidden, is revealed (Gk. *mystērion*; Mk 4:11; 1 Cor 2:7; 15:51; Eph 3:3-10; Ign., *Eph.* 19.1; *Magn.* 9.1).

mystery plays. Late medieval *dramas portraying scriptural events, especially the life of Christ, usually organized and performed by *lay organizations and performed outside of the church service, though perhaps originally influenced by the liturgy.

mystery religion. An ancient individual-oriented salvation cult (see Burkert) surrounding a particular deity who undergoes change, even death (see Sfameni Gasparro). Though differing from each other in notable ways, the mystery *cults tended to have a number of characteristics in common, namely secretive nocturnal initiations (perhaps involving a subterranean experience), identification of the initiate with the sufferings of a particular deity, implied rebirth (e.g., Apuleius, *Metamorphoses* 11.21: *renatos*, "born again"), change in status of the initiate as Fate had been overcome (cf. *Metamorphoses* 11.15, 16, 25; *Excerpta ex Theodoto* 78) and the hope of a blessed afterlife (see Burkert). The cultic settings of Mithraism (*mithraea*) frequently took on a cave-like subterranean motif, grain emerging from the tail of the slain bull in the famous central *iconography (see Ulansey [A]).

Ancient Christian *baptism has parallels with *mystery *cult initiations in, for example, nocturnal environment, identification with a deity who undergoes death, a new birth and even new clothes (c.f. Apuleius, *Metamorphoses* 11.24). Cyril of Jerusalem regarded baptism as mystery initiation (*Myst. Cat.* 1.1). On the other hand, baptismal language is also indicative of OT redemptive sacrifice (*see* Paschal Lamb).

The entrance to the *Dura-Europos *baptistery displays what Kraeling has noted to be the first four letters of the Greek alphabet followed by a star ("A B Γ Δ *"), and he associates these figures with the *stoicheia*, Greek for "basic elements," because *stoicheia* can refer to both the alphabet (cf. Heb 5:12) and the celestial elements (cf. 2 Pet 3:10, 12). Paul wrote, after addressing baptism's mitigation of social categories (Gal 3:26-29), that the Christian is no longer subject to the *stoicheia* (Gal 4:3, 9, "elemental spirits"; cf. Col 2:8-13, 15, 20). Such a liberation may be reflected in Jesus' baptism and the *tearing apart* of the heavens (Mk 1:10), such a rending corresponding to the *tearing into two* the veil of the temple at Jesus' death (Mk 15:38), the temple veil itself having on it a representation of the heavens (Josephus, *Jewish War* 5.5.4; see Ulansey [B]).

N

narthex. The congregation's entrance to the *nave.

nave. A central part of the *church building interior; the place where the congregation is situated. The church building in function, even at times in form, is analogous to a ship, which is the derivation of this term (Lat. *navis*; Gk. *naus*). See the appendix.

Neander, Joachim (1789-1850). A German hymnist who wrote the famous hymn "Praise to the Lord, the Almighty" (Eng. translation). In a valley (Ger. *thal*) named after him were discovered the famous Neanderthal bones.

New Testament. The portion of the Christian *canon of sacred Scripture (originally written in Greek) that centers around the person and work of *Jesus Christ and the religious interests and activities of his early followers. The New Testament and the *Old

Testament together (as well as the *Apocrypha for some) form the complete canon of the Christian Bible. Part of the NT is always read in both the *Liturgy of the Word and the *Daily Office.

New Year's Day. The first day of a new year. In the history of religions New Year's celebrations are nearly ubiquitous, with New Year's envisioned as the time when the world is (re)created, a new cosmic birth recognized. (The first two chapters of Genesis have been thought by some to be related to New Year's liturgies of the ancient Near East.) Depending on the culture, the new year may begin in the spring (especially near the *equinox), in the fall (e.g., the civil year in the OT) or near the winter *solstice (the birth of the new sun), or even at some other time. Often a period of chaos precedes the new year, such as carnival, the period just before the beginning of the *Lenten season that precedes *Easter.

New Year's Day (January 1) is the *octave (eighth day) of *Christmas and thus commemorates the *Circumcision of Jesus. The day was also long ago associated with the birth of the Virgin *Mary.

Nicene Creed. The *confession of faith originated at the *Council of Nicaea (325) and noteworthy for its trinitarian and christological formulations. Later confirmed and modified (perhaps at the Council of Constantinople in 381), it is generally considered the primary statement of Christian orthodoxy and the doctrinal basis for Christian *unity.

Nicholas, St. (c. late second century–early third century). A bishop of Myra, said to be a fiery defender of the *Athanasian understanding of the incarnation and a participant at the *Council of Nicaea. He was well known for assisting needy children and being generally benevolent, a reputation that finds him later mythologized into the roving benefactor of *Christmas, Santa Claus (*Claus* being a rendering of *Nicholas*). He is the patron saint of Greece and Russia, and his feast day is December 6.

night. The daily period of darkness sanctified in Christian liturgy by the *vigils of the church. *See also* Compline.

Night Prayer. *See* Compline.

Nocturns. From Latin *nocturnus*, "of the night" (Lat. *nox*, "night"), an early-morning *office of *prayer (about midnight on) historically associated with *Matins (in fact, *Nocturns* is also a term for the sections of Matins). In the EC, Ps 133 (LXX) and Is 26:9-11 are recited; in the WC, Ps 95 (94). Also known as *Vigils, the *Office of

Readings today fulfills this Hour in the RC *Liturgy of the Hours.*

Noonday Prayer. *See* Daily Office.

Notre Dame, Paris. An early *Gothic *cathedral whose beginning dates to 1163. It is dedicated to the Virgin *Mary (Fr. *Notre Dame,* "Our Lady"), as are a number of French Gothic cathedrals (e.g., Amiens and Chartres). It is built on the Île de la Cité in the Seine River in the heart of Paris.

Notre-Dame du Raincy. A modern *church building designed by Auguste Perret (1923), considered the first designed as a result of the *liturgical renewal, its open interior having the *altar closer and clearly visible to the *laity (see Hammond).

numbers, special. Numbers that have religious significance (e.g.): 1 = the unity of God and the *unity of the body of Christ; 3 = the Holy *Trinity; 7 = completion; 8 = new beginning; 12 = ideal governance; 40 = trial or testing.

nun. From Latin *nonna,* a term of honor meaning "mother," a woman who has taken *religious orders, often associated with a *monastery. In ancient Christianity nuns were also referred to as *parthenae* (*"virgins").

Nunc Dimittis. The first words (in Latin) of the song the aged Simeon sings upon seeing the infant Jesus during his presentation in the temple (Lk 2:29-32). Appropriate at *Candlemas and after *Communion, it has also for many centuries (since at least the *Apostolic Constitutions*) been recited at *Vespers and *Compline (RC).

O

"O" Antiphons. Well-known *plainsong *antiphons for the *Advent season. In English "O Come, O Come, Emmanuel" (Latin *Veni, veni, Emanuel*) is an example. The Dorian *mode musical setting familiar today probably dates to the twelfth or thirteenth century, while there is evidence that much of the text dates at least to the time of Charlemagne (c. 800). Intended for *Vespers, a different verse is sung each evening of *Advent beginning December 17, and an acrostic is formed from the first letter of the appellation of Jesus in each of these seven antiphons (i.e., "O Sapientia . . . Adonai . . . Radix . . . Clavis . . . Oriens . . . Rex . . . Emanuel"), SARCORE, which reversed is the Latin expression *ero cras,* "I will be [present] tomorrow," an appropriate promise from the Savior to those who, anticipating his coming, sing the song through the evening of December 23 (see Keyte and Parrott). Translated from Latin: *Sapientia*, "Wisdom"; *Adonai*, Hebrew for "Lord"; *Radix*, "Root [of Jesse]"; *Clavis*, "Key [of David]"; *Oriens*, "Rising Sun" or "Dayspring"; *Rex*, "King"; and *Emanuel*, Hebrew for "God with us" (Mt 1:23; Is 7:14). These special seven days of Advent are known as Sapientiatide.

"O Come, O Come, Emmanuel." *See* "O" Antiphons.

O Sapientia (December 17). A day commemorating Jesus as Wisdom (Lat. *sapientia:* 1 Cor 1:30). This day begins the progressive *"O" Antiphons.

oblation. An *offering. When used of the *eucharistic *bread, it is synonymous with Greek *prosphora* (a term used concerning Jesus' death at Eph 5:2; Heb 10:10, 14).

occasional offices. Also known as pastoral offices, those irregularly occurring *rites such as for marriage, the sick and burial.

octagon. A common shape of earlier Christian *baptisteries and *fonts beginning in the fourth century. The shape is perhaps preferred due to the "eight" persons saved in Noah's ark (1 Pet 3:20-21), though the octagon was also used in pagan funerary design (e.g., the tomb of the emperor Diocletian).

octave. Literally "the eighth [day]," the day exactly one week following certain feast days. The octave of *Christmas is January 1 (*see* Circumcision of Christ, Feast of the).

offering. The gifts of the people to God. Members of the *laity often bring the collected gifts forward in worship. Historically the offering precedes the *Liturgy of the Eucharist (*see* offertory), the wine and bread for the service presented by congregants as an *oblation. Some churches have the offering follow the Eucharist as an act of gratitude toward God's saving work (*see* Reformed order of worship), and some churches have the offering before the *lessons and *sermon.

offertory. The part of the liturgy where the gifts of the people are presented (*see* offering). The offertory is quite ancient (*Ap. Trad.* 4.2; 21.27). Some scholars find allusions to the Eucharist in the accounts of the feedings with loaves and *fish in the *Gospels (e.g., Mk 6:32-44; 8:1-9). If such is the case, then the acquisition of the initial loaves and fish from someone present (Jn 6:9) is a parallel to the church's offertory. Interestingly, the ancient *Apostolic Tradition* also notes offerings of oil (5), cheese and olives (6), as well as milk, honey and water (21.28-29). The term *offertory* also applies to any music accompanying this part of the liturgy.

office. A prescribed service of worship (*see*, e.g., Daily Office).

Office, Daily. *See* Daily Office.

Office for the Dead. A special office for honoring the dead in the RC. Parts of the Office are quite ancient. Only certain hours were recognized in the old RC *breviary (*Vespers on the *eve, *Matins and *Lauds, i.e., not a "daytime" office), though this is not the case in the recent *Liturgy of the Hours*. Especially appropriate on All Souls' Day (*see* All Saints' Day).

Office of Readings. In the RC what used to be known as *Matins. It differs from other *offices in that it includes an extended reading from a recognized figure in Christian history and may be recited at any time of the day or night. Analogous is the *CW* Prayer During the Day, which includes "quiet time and Bible study."

officiant. One who presides over a *formal ritual gathering.

oil. A substance for *sealing a new convert, *symbolic of the *Holy Spirit. *See also* anoint; chrism.

Old Roman Creed. The ancient version (late second century) of what is now known as the *Apostles' Creed. A *baptismal *confession of the church at Rome, it has been preserved in the *Apostolic Tradition* (21.12-17), the three-part creed corresponding to *trine immersion in the name of the *Trinity. Its elements are anticipated in NT statements of belief (e.g., Rom 1:3-4; 8:34; 1 Cor 15:3-5; 1 Tim 6:13-14; 1 Pet 3:18-20; see Kelly).

Old St. Peter's (Rome). The *basilica originally built by Constantine on the Vatican Hill in Rome (dedicated 324). Orientated toward the *west, it was originally funerary in purpose, a place where Christians gathered to honor the deceased (*see refrigerium*). This historically important building was gradually demolished, beginning in 1506 (by order of Pope Julius II), to make way for the current *St. Peter's Basilica, much to the chagrin of some, including Michelangelo, who ironically designed the great *dome for the current structure.

Old Testament. The portion of the *canon of Christian Scripture written in Hebrew and Aramaic that emerged within ancient Israelite and Jewish religion and is often referred to as the Hebrew

Bible. This body of sacred literature (in Heb. called *Tanakh*) was intrinsic to nascent Christianity and thus forms a great part of the Christian Bible. Today a selection from the OT is often read as part of the *Liturgy of the Word. In the *Daily Office of the *ABCP* much of the OT is read annually in the course of *Morning and *Evening Prayers.

orans. Found frequently in ancient Christian funerary art, a human figure with hands reaching upward in a prayerful or joyous manner (Lat. *oro*, "to pray").

oratorio. A choral work, often religious in nature, incorporating arias, recitatives and choruses. It is the nontheatrical counterpart to *opera*.

order of worship. The standard *rite for any service of worship, including *Sunday worship, *baptism, *funeral, *ordination, the *Daily Office, etc. Traditionally a WC Sunday order of worship includes much of what is show in table 4, both in approximate order and content, and is divided into two dominant parts: the *Liturgy of the Word and the *Liturgy of the Eucharist.

Table 4. Common Components of Worship in a Western Church

Prelude	
Opening/entrance/convocation	Call to worship
	Hymn of procession or hymn of praise
	Invocation
	God's greeting to his people
Preparation/reconciliation	Confession of sin and absolution/penitential rite
	Kyrie Eleison
	Gloria in Excelsis Deo
	Collect/prayer for illumination
Liturgy of the Word	(see entry)
Offering/offertory	Offering
Liturgy of the Eucharist	(see entry)
Conclusion/dismissal	Prayer of thanksgiving
	Doxology
	Benediction
Postlude	

order, religious. A *clerical or *religious group involving *vows and sometimes *ordination (e.g., Dominicans, Jesuits).

ordinal. A liturgical *order of worship and/or *readings, or a book containing such, for ordaining (e.g.) *bishops, *priests and *deacons.

ordinance. A term used for the *rites of *baptism and the *Eucharist by some Protestants who hold that grace is not conveyed by these two rites. These purely *symbolic rites are called *ordinances* because they were *ordained* by Jesus; *obedient* participation is thereby demanded (cf. BF&M 6-7).

Ordinary. As distinct from the *Proper, the unchanging parts of the liturgy (e.g., the *Sanctus and the *Lord's Prayer).

Ordinary Time. In the RC those parts of the *liturgical year not part of *Advent, the *Christmas season, *Lent or *Eastertide; in other words, usually between *Epiphany (or the *Baptism of Our Lord) and *Ash Wednesday, and the long period from the day after *Pentecost *Sunday to the beginning of Advent. The name derives from the *ordinal* numbering of the Sundays and their respective weeks. Many other denominations also recognize this time, the Sundays often termed, for example, "the *n* Sunday after Pentecost" or "Proper *n*." Color: green.

ordination rites. The *rites pertaining to the ordination (*consecration) of *clergy and *lay officials.

ordo. Latin for "order," the RC liturgical *calendar with certain specifics given for *Mass, the *offices and special days of observance. A similar calendar in the OC is called the *Typikon*.

organ. A traditional musical instrument that accompanies corporate singing in churches. Appearing in the Middle Ages (more as complement than accompaniment to the *choir), its rise to prominence occurred during the Renaissance, especially at *St. Mark's Cathedral in Venice under the influence of Adriaan Willaert and the *Gabrielis. Electronic amplification has allowed for other instruments to accompany corporate singing in churches today.

organum. Latin meaning "tool" or "instrument," an *organum* involves medieval *plainsong developed into *polyphony* ("many voices") by adding a second line (or more) of corresponding melody to an already established line of melody. *See also cantus firmus.*

Our Modern Services (2002). The *liturgical book of the Anglican Church of Kenya, a notable example of *inculturation as it merges much of the *ABCP* tradition with African cultural distinctives, interests and needs (see LeMarquand).

P

Palestrina, Giovanni (c. 1525-1594). An important RC composer of the Counter-Reformation whose work is characterized by clear, straightforward melodies.

pall. From Latin *pallium*, "a cover," a black cloth placed over a funerary casket, but sometimes white (representative of the deceased's *baptismal *robe). The term also applies to the cloth (stiffened with a board) that covers the *eucharistic *chalice.

Palm Sunday. The first day of *Holy Week, commemorating Jesus' triumphal entry into Jerusalem (Mk 11:1-11; Mt 21:1-11; Lk 19:28-40; Jn 12:12-19). It was celebrated in Jerusalem as early as the late fourth century. In the *Byzantine Rite, the day before Palm Sunday is *Lazarus Saturday. Color: violet or red.

Pantocrator. A Greek term translated "Almighty" in the first line of the *Apostles' Creed. In *Byzantine art it is applied to representations of Jesus where above his head a cross pattern is inscribed within a halo, with Jesus often set as the central figure in a heavenly *dome. This central position is related to the concept of the *polokratōr*, "the ruler of the [celestial] pole," around whom the starry canopy of heaven rotates (the pole located near the seven stars of Ursa Major). This position of sovereign power (even over fate) was accorded certain heroes: Hercules (Seneca, *Hercules Oetaeus* 1940-41), Mithras (*PGM* 4.692-704), Perseus (Hippolytus, *Refutation of All Heresies* 5.44) and Jesus (Rev 1:16; cf. 1 Cor 15:25-26; see Malina; Ulansey [A]). In the *cubicula* of the Roman *catacombs Jesus is frequently portrayed as the *Good Shepherd in the center ring of a *dome of heaven motif.

paraments. Cloth adornments for liturgical furniture (e.g., *pulpit scarf, *Communion table runner), the *colors corresponding to the liturgical season or occasion.

Pascha Nostrum (Christ Our Passover). A liturgical text made up of 1 Corinthians 5:7-8, Romans 6:9-11 and 1 Corinthians 15:20-22. Especially appropriate during *Eastertide, it is also known as the "Easter Anthems" (*CW*).

Pascha, Pasch. From Hebrew *pesach*, "Passover," the ancient Christian name for *Passover, especially as it takes on the commemoration of the death and resurrection of Jesus Christ. It runs from the *vigil beginning Holy Saturday evening on through all of *Easter Sunday. The term in the EC also refers to *Eastertide. *See also* Paschal Vigil.

Paschal candle. A special *candle lit during the darkness of the *Paschal Vigil, *symbolizing Jesus' victory over death. It also may be part of *baptismal and *funerary services.

Paschal Lamb. The redemptive lamb sacrificed at *Passover which Christians identify with Jesus (1 Cor 5:7; Rev 5:6 and passim; cf. Mk 14:12; Lk 22:7-8; cf. also Jn 19:32, 36 with the stricture against breaking bones at Ex 12:46). The NT holds that *redemption,* the *sacrifice of one victim in the place of another (cf. Ex 13:13; 34:19-20), is through Christ's blood: Christ is the *redeeming* sacrifice (Rom 3:24-25; Eph 1:7; Col 1:13-14; 1 Pet 1:18-19; cf. Mk 10:45; 2 Cor 5:14-15; Gal 3:13-14). It is this redemptive sacrificial death that is celebrated at the *Eucharist and at *Maundy Thursday and *Good Friday of *Holy Week.

Specifically, sacrifice of the firstborn was commanded in the OT (Ex 13:2; cf. 22:29-30) and fulfilled in the redemptive Passover sacrifice (Ex 13:13-15). A like demand was made of Abraham for his only, beloved one (Heb. *yāhîd*; Gk. *agapētos*), Isaac (Gen 22:2, 16), who was redeemed with a ram (see Levenson). Jesus too was designated *only, beloved* and *firstborn* (Mk 1:11; Lk 2:7; Jn 3:16; Rom 8:29, 32; Heb 1:6; 11:28; Rev 1:7 w. Zech 12:10-12; see Levenson), and thus as "the firstborn of all creation" became the redemptive sacrifice not only on behalf of humanity but of all *creation (Col 1:15, 18-20).

At some point the sacrifice of the firstborn or beloved became associated with atonement for sin (cf. Mic 6:7). Thus atonement for sin, usually in the OT associated with sin and guilt offerings (Lev 4:1-35; 5:14–6:7; 7:1-7) or with the Day of Atonement sacrifice (Lev 16), was acknowledged in Jesus' death (Rom 3:23-25a; 5:6-11; 2 Cor 5:21; Eph 1:7; Col 1:13-14; Heb 7:27; 9:11-15; cf. Is 53:4-6, 10-12, likely associated with Passover). Indeed, Jesus at the beginning of his ministry is identified both with the redemptive sacrificial language applied to Isaac (Mk 1:11; Lk 3:22; cf. Gen 22:2, 16; Judg 11:29-31, 34-35; 2 Kings 3:26-27; see Levenson) and with the atoning Lamb (Jn 1:29, 36; cf. Is 53:7, 12; CCC 536).

This sacrificial language also applies to the believer in *baptism (cf. Mk 1:4; Acts 2:38), concepts such as *beloved, firstborn, redemption, blood* and *sonship*, as well as vicarious death and forgiveness of sins, used to elucidate the baptismal status of Christians (e.g., Eph 1:3-14, esp. 5-7, 13; Col 1:13-14, 18-22; Rev 1:5-6 with 7:14; 1 Pet 1:18-23; see Osten-Sacken). Indeed, baptismal martyrdom and the altar of the Lamb are drawn together (Rev 6:9). Christians are, therefore, ritually identified with Jesus Christ.

Paschal Vigil. Historically the most important annual liturgical service in Christianity. Beginning the evening of *Holy Saturday, it is celebrated in high liturgical traditions, and its roots certainly precede its earliest extant manifestation (*Ap. Trad.* 20.9 passim, if indeed it is Paschal liturgy given there).

The service begins with the *Paschal candle, then *readings are prominent and noteworthy for OT types reflecting baptismal nuances (table 5 summarizes the Scripture readings in the *EBCP*). The *vigil traditionally concludes with the *baptism of *catechumens and their first *Communion.

Table 5. Scripture Readings for Paschal Vigil

Creation	Gen 1:1-2:2	Ps 33:1-11	or	Ps 36:5-10
Flood	Gen 7:1-5, 11-18; 8:6-18; 9:8-13	Ps 46		
Sacrifice of Isaac	Gen 22:1-18	Ps 33:12-22	or	Ps 16
Red Sea	Ex 14:10–15:1	Song of Moses		
God's Presence	Is 4:2-6	Ps 122		
Salvation Offered	Is 55:1-11	First *Song of Isaiah	or	Ps 42:1-7
New Creation of Individual	Ezek 36:24-28	Ps 42:1-7	or	First Song of Isaiah
Dry Bones	Ezek 37:1-14	Ps 30	or	Ps 143
Gathering	Zeph 3:12-20	Ps 98	or	Ps 126

Passion. The period of suffering Jesus endured in the final hours of his earthly ministry (related to Gk. *pathos*; Lat. *passio*, "suffering"). Liturgically a *Passion* is a musical setting of a Gospel narrative of Jesus' Passion. Notable are *Bach's *St. Matthew's Passion* and *St.*

John's Passion, the former including the melody of the somber yet noble hymn "O Sacred Head, Now Wounded." *See also* Holy Week.

Passover. A springtime Jewish *feast (*Pesach*) commemorating the liberation of the Hebrew slaves from Egyptian bondage (Ex 12:43-50; 13:1-16; Deut 16:1-8). The OT story involves the evening sacrifice of *Paschal lambs, the nocturnal family *vigil (juxtaposed to the nocturnal visitation of death), and the ensuing morning release of the children of Israel (Ex 12:1-32). Often the crossing of the Red Sea is included within Passover imagery (Ex 14), and *Psalms 113–118 (the Egyptian Hallel) are associated with this *holy feast (see Ps 114).

In the Torah, the Paschal Lamb was to be sacrificed on the fourteenth of the month of Nisan (Ex 12:6), which falls variously year to year sometime within March or April. In the NT, the Passover becomes the backdrop for the *Passion of Jesus Christ (Mk 14:12; Lk 22:7-8), and early Christians such as *Melito of Sardis made a phonetic connection between *Pascha* (Passover) and *paschō* (Gk. meaning "to suffer," and thus conceptually *passion*). Significantly *baptism came to be understood as the fulfillment of the crossing of the Red Sea (1 Cor 10:1-2), Christians noting their own release from the bonds of sin and the devil in Christ's Passion. *See also* Last Supper.

The OT story follows a pattern familiar in the history of religions (*see* mystery religion), and it is thus not surprising that the Passover was understood as a mystery by Melito in his *Peri Pascha*. Indeed, the Passover story has elements in common with a mystery *rite (e.g., nocturnal vigil, confrontation with death, new status the following morning).

pastor. From Latin for "shepherd," derived from *pasco*, "to feed," the title or position of a ranking *minister with the idea that the minister is shepherd of the congregational flock (cf. Jn 21:15-17). Often preferred as a title to the more formal "Reverend."

pastoral offices. *See* occasional offices.

pastoral prayer. The corporate *prayer of thanksgiving and *petition led or given by the *minister on behalf of the congregation. It may be extemporaneous as well as prescribed or traditional. *See also* prayers of the people.

paten. From Latin *patina*, "pan," the plate on which the *eucharistic *bread is placed at the *Communion *table.

Patrick, Prayer of St. Often referred to as "St. Patrick's Breastplate," a morning prayer characterized by *creed, appreciation of *creation, the need for divine protection and the presence of Christ. The prayer has been attributed to the *evangelist and *bishop St. Patrick (died latter half of fifth century), a Christian from Britain who took the gospel to Ireland, of which he is the patron saint. His feast day is March 17.

Paul, Conversion of (January 25). The feast commemorating Paul's conversion on the Damascus Road (Acts 9:1-19; 22:4-16; 26:9-18). A feast to Paul is sometimes celebrated on June 30.

peace, the. (Heb. *šālôm*; Gk. *eirēnē*; Lat. *pax*). A practice that fulfills the exhortation that Christians greet one another with a holy kiss (Rom 16:16). Given cultural differences in personal space, this is also fulfilled through handshakes and other forms of public welcome and greetings. The peace is a joyous part of the worship service, sometimes following the *confession of sin and *declaration of forgiveness (cf. Is 53:5) or some other point before or during the *Liturgy of the Eucharist. Inscriptions bearing the word *peace* are often indicative of Christian burial in the Roman *catacombs. *See also* Kiss of Peace.

penance. A formal act concerned with *confession of sin to a priest and, ultimately, restoration. It is a *sacrament in the RC ("Confession").

Penitential Order. A *rite of examination, *confession and *absolution (called "An Order for Preparation" in *CW*) that precedes the *Liturgy of the Word. In Protestant liturgies it is optional, and not conducted if confession of sin and absolution are part of the service.

Pentecost. From Greek *pentēkostos* "fiftieth," a major feast celebrated in churches on *Whitsunday and celebrating the giving of the Holy Spirit to the Jerusalem disciples. Pentecost comes fifty days after *Passover, falling on the sixth of the ancient Jewish month Sivan, which is the end of the barley harvest (Lev 23:15-21). It was one of the three major feasts of the OT (Deut 16:16), called the Feast of Weeks (Jewish Shovuos, which later became the feast commemorating the giving of the *Law). This time was also the beginning of the wheat harvest (Ex 34:22), and thus the feast is an agricultural harvest festival characterized by the offering of two loaves of wheat *bread.

For the Christian church it was on Pentecost that the *Holy Spirit filled the gathered disciples of Jesus in the Jerusalem temple precinct, empowering them to proclaim and elucidate the gospel of Jesus of Nazareth (Acts 2:1-11, 22-36). Three thousand people were converted and baptized, and thus that day is often recognized as the birthday of the church (Acts 2:41; cf. Ex 32:28). The day maintained significance for Christians in the NT (1 Cor 16:8; Acts 20:16) as well as for the postapostolic church, functioning as the final high point of *Eastertide begun on *Easter Sunday.

Today the months following Pentecost complete the *liturgical year, ending the day before *Advent season begins. Since the first part of the liturgical year focuses on the life of Jesus, the second part (post-Pentecost) focuses on Christ working in his church. In some traditions *Pentecost* in fact is the name of the long period between the Day of Pentecost and Advent. Color: red or white. *See also* Ordinary Time.

Pentecostal worship. Worship characteristic of churches in the Pentecostal movement. Often influenced by the *revival service of worship as well as the Wesleyan/Holiness tradition (out of which a number of Pentecostal denominations emerged), Pentecostal worship is further distinguished by the addition of the intensified experience of the *charismata (including healing) and Spirit-led *spontaneity (cf. 2 Cor 3:17), including *baptism in the Holy Spirit.

pericope. From the Greek word meaning "section," a particular portion of Scripture to be read as a *lesson. Certain ancient manuscripts of the NT, such as Vaticanus and Alexandrinus, have the NT marked into pericopes, and liturgical *readings are attested as early as Justin (*1 Apol.* 67). *See also* kephalaia.

Peter and Paul, Feast of Apostles (June 29). A day commemorating the two paramount apostles, the former to the Jews, the latter to the Gentiles (Gal 2:7), though some traditions recognize only Peter on this day. These two figures were linked as far back as *1 Clem.* 5, which holds up the two as paradigms of suffering for Christ. Tradition has Peter buried on the Vatican Hill beneath *St. Peter's Basilica, and in the mid-twentieth century the second-century memorial to Peter (Eusebius, *Ecclesiastical History* 2.25) was discovered directly beneath the high altar of the current basilica. *Paul was buried along the Ostian Way at Rome (*Basilica of St. Paul Outside the Walls). Beginning about the mid-third century the two were joined in epigraphic *petitions at a particular section of the Roman *catacombs known as Ad Catacumbas, which is beneath the church of S. Sebastiano along the Appian Way. Peter and Paul are patron *saints of Rome.

petition. A *prayer requesting something of a deity. The *Lord's Prayer has seven *petitions*. Also called a *suffrage*.

Philip, Feast of (June 6). A day commemorating Philip the *evangelist who was based in Caesarea and had four prophesying *virgin daughters (Acts 21:8-9). He was one of the original *deacons of the nascent church (Acts 6:5). He is not the same person as Philip the apostle, whose EC feast day (Nov. 14) immediately precedes the beginning of EC *Advent (called the Fast of St. Philip).

Philip Neri (1515-1595). A Counter-Reformation activist who encouraged the development of the musical form known as *oratorio.

philos. Greek for "beloved," "friend," one who partakes with others in a Greco-Roman meal (*see* Aberkios Inscription).

Phos Hilaron. An ancient *hymn of the church that is part of the evening lamp-lighting service (*see* service of light), or recited at *Evening Prayer (especially in the EC). A number of Protestant service books have now included a special service of light in which the hymn is sung.

O gracious Light [*Phōs hilaron*],
pure brightness of the everliving Father in heaven,
O Jesus Christ, holy and blessed!

Now as we come to the setting of the sun,
and our eyes behold the vesper light,
we sing your praises, O God: Father, Son and Holy Spirit.

You are worthy at all times to be praised by happy voices,
O Son of God, O Giver of Life,
and to be glorified through all the worlds. (*EBCP*)

pilgrimage. A journey to a particular religious site as a special act of religious devotion or penance. Pilgrimages were especially popular during the Middle Ages, taken on foot with others in company to sites associated with the resting places or relics of various saints (cf. Chaucer's *Canterbury Tales*). The most popular destinations were the Holy Land, Rome and the church of *Santiago de Compostela in Spain.

plainsong. A liturgical vocal *chant in the WC composed of a single line of melody, often sung in unison with others, having neither *meter nor instrumental accompaniment. *See also* Gregorian chant.

postlude. The music played at the end of a worship service, especially to accompany the people exiting the church.

Praetorius, Michael (1571-1621). A German Lutheran music scholar and composer of *hymn tunes and settings, including "Lo, How a Rose E'er Blooming" and "Good Christian Men, Rejoice!"

praise. Words that glorify God (derived from Lat. *pretium*, "value"; cf. Heb. verb *hālal*). Often set to music, praise is the congregation's response to God's gifts and majesty (Heb 13:15; also Ps 50:14; cf. Rom 12:1).

praise music. Also known as *praise and worship music*, music for *contemporary corporate worship rooted in the *Pentecostal/charismatic-inspired Jesus People Movement (e.g., Calvary Chapel and Vineyard churches). Some songs set Scripture to music; other original compositions may stress a deeply personal mood and purpose with devotionally emotive, even kinetic, energy. In practice, singing may tend toward choruses sung repetitively. The congregational singing is often led by a *worship team, and the music might also be interlaced with prayers and exclamations of faith. Strongly composed within, and directed toward, popular music preferences, praise music finds a place today in more and more churches. Implementation is technologically inclined, frequently incorporating a multimedia experience, lending itself well to the *revival service of worship. Indeed, "worship" in some churches may be defined as the music portion of the Sunday service.

prayer. From Latin *precor*, "to beseech," words addressed to a deity, taking on various forms such as *praise, thanksgiving, *petition, *supplication and *intercession. In the liturgy there may be both fixed prayers and others freely constructed (extempore prayer).

There are many prayers in the Bible, including those of the *Psalter, and many of these have been incorporated in Christian liturgies. Jesus frequently prays in the Gospels; Paul exhorts to "pray without ceasing" (1 Thess 5:17). In the NT prayer is frequently addressed to God the Father through Jesus Christ his Son

(2 Cor 1:3; 1 Pet 1:3; Rom 1:8), and this carries on in later writings (e.g., *1 Clem.* 61.3; *Ap. Trad.* 4.4, 13).

Christian liturgical prayers include the *Lord's Prayer, many of the *canticles, the *Eucharistic Prayer and the *prayers of the people. Whole services are also referred to as *prayers* (*see* Daily Office; Morning Prayer; Evening Prayer).

prayer for illumination. The *officiant's prayer for the guidance of the *Holy Spirit in understanding the *readings (*see* Calvin, John).

prayer meeting. *See* midweek service.

Prayer of Humble Access. Words said in the *ABCP* after the *Sanctus and just before the *Eucharistic Prayer, and in the *EBCP* (Holy Eucharist I) after the *Agnus Dei. Retained by some Methodist churches.

prayer of the day. *See* collect.

prayers of the people. Similar to the pastoral prayer, it includes thanksgivings, *petitions and *intercessions on behalf of believers and the world at large (1 Tim 2:1-4). In the higher liturgies the *minister might say intermittingly "Lord, in your mercy," and the people complete with "hear our prayer." Some churches allow individuals to come forward with petitions and needs at this time.

preacher. Someone who publicly declares and expounds the *Word of God (Rom 10:17), particularly the gospel message (Rom 10:14-15; 1 Cor 15:1-4), the *kērygma* (Rom 16:25; 1 Cor 1:21).

preces. Plural of Latin *prex*, "prayer" said *responsively.

preface. From Latin *praefatio*, "proclamation," (1) the first section of the eucharistic *Anaphora, which includes the *Sursum Corda and the *Sanctus; and (2) the *prayer, variable in the WC (the Proper Preface), that is part of (1).

prelude. A piece of music played before the beginning of the worship service. Its purpose is to help prepare the congregation for worship.

presbyter. From Greek *presbyteros*, "elder," a leadership office of the church. The nature of the position varies widely among the denominations, from ordained *clergy (e.g., the RC, as the word *priest* is cognate to *presbyter*) to *lay elders in many Protestant denominations, and even among these roles vary.

presbyterian. Churches ruled by a group of *elders rather than a single *bishop or the *congregation; associated with the Calvinist tradition.

Presentation of Christ. *See* Candlemas.

priest. The ordained *clergy (from Gk. *presbyteros,* "elder") within the RC, AC and LC, ranking lower than a *bishop.

procession. A formal entrance. In the OC there are two entrances: (1) the Little Entrance opening the Liturgy of the *Catechumens; (2) the Great Entrance opening the Liturgy of the Faithful, in which the *ministers bring the *eucharistic *bread and *wine from the prothesis (where they were prepared) to the *altar. These two parts of the OC service (Liturgies of the Catechumens and of the Faithful) parallel the WC *Liturgy of the Word and *Liturgy of the Eucharist (see Wybrew). In the WC the opening procession may involve the ministers and assistants. The person who carries the cross, often leading the procession, is the *crucifer.

proper. Variable elements of liturgies such as *prayers, *psalms and *lessons assigned to a particular *Sunday, *holy day or season (e.g., the Proper for Epiphany). Proper parts of the *Mass include, for example, the *Introit, the *Gradual and the *Offertory.

psalm. A religious or sacred song (from Gk. *psalmos,* a song accompanied by a harp). *See also* Psalter.

psalm tones. A medieval innovation associating the *modes with recitation of *psalms. There are eight tones in all.

psalmody. In the *Daily Office, the section in which the *psalms are read, including assigned *antiphons and *Gloria Patris (and psalm-prayers in the RC).

Psalter. The OT book of *Psalms, which contains the liturgical *prayers and songs of the Jewish people, generally categorized as *hymns (songs of praise), thanksgivings and laments. The hymns focus on God's creative and saving acts (e.g., Ps 8; 19; 33; 104; 111; 113; 135–136).

In the Jewish tradition, the Psalter is divided into five *books*, each ending with a *doxology (Ps 41; 72; 89; 106; 150). Important *series* of psalms include (1) the Great Hallel (Ps 120–136), which includes the *pilgrimage Psalms of Ascent (Ps 120–134, the "Gradual Psalms"); (2) the Egyptian Hallel recited at *Passover and new *moons (Ps 113–118); and (3) the Hallel (Ps 146–150), which includes the *Laudes* of the later Christian *Daily Office. *Weekly* morning psalms sung in the Jerusalem temple were (according to the Talmud) Psalms 24 (Sunday), 48 (Monday), 82 (Tuesday), 94 (Wednesday), 81 (Thursday), 93 (Friday), 92 (Sabbath/Saturday), a pattern applicable to corresponding days of creation in Genesis 1 and 2.

The psalms, being a key component of Christian worship as well, are always prayed in the *Daily Office. Recitation of the Psalter in the *EBCP* follows a seven-week cycle; the RC, *ABCP* and LC follow a four-week cycle. Originally in the WC the Psalter was read through in its entirety every week in the *monastery office.

In the various offices, historically typical *morning* psalms include 3, 51, 63, 67, 100, 148–150, 113:3 (e. Syrian), whereas *evening* psalms include 4, 104, 134, 141, 143. The lengthy Psalm 119 was recited during the night *vigil (see Taft).

Representative musical settings: *Traditional:* "All People That on Earth Do Dwell," the "Old 100th" (Ps 100); "Bless the Lord, O My Soul" (Ps 103); *Paraphrased:* "Our God Our Help in Ages Past" (Ps 90); *Revival:* "This Is the Day" (Ps 118); *Contemporary/Praise:* "As the Deer" (Ps 42); "Sing a Joyful Song" (Ps 100); *Derived:* "A Mighty Fortress Is Our God" (Ps 46). *See also* Jubilate; Venite.

pulpit. The place from which the main *reading and teaching of the Scripture occurs in the church service. It is prominent in the P&RC, where it is often spatially elevated.

Q

Quadragesima. Latin for "fortieth," (1) the *Lenten season of forty days, and specifically (2) the first Sunday of Lent.

Quartodeciman. From Latin for "fourteen," a label for any Christian in the early church who celebrated the *Pascha (*Easter) on the fourteenth of Nisan (*see* Passover), a day that falls on a different day of the week from year to year. A controversy took place in the second century between the Quartodecimans and other Christians, particularly at Rome, who demanded that Easter be celebrated the first *Sunday *following* the fourteenth. The well-known second-century *bishop and theologian Irenaeus, though in agreement with Roman observance, wrote an important letter to the bishop of Rome encouraging him to take a position of tolerance. Quartodecimans counted among their number Polycarp and *Melito of Sardis, the latter writing an important liturgical work for the Pascha.

Quicunque Vult. Latin title for the *Athanasian Creed.

Quinquagesima. Latin for "fiftieth," the *Sunday before the beginning of *Lent.

quire. *See* choir.

R

rail, altar. Also known as the Communion rail, the liminal fence surrounding the precinct of the *altar at which *communicants *kneel or *stand to receive the *Eucharist. In some traditions, crossing the *threshold of the rail is performed with *reverence (e.g., bowing). *See also* iconostasis; sacred space.

Ravenna. A city near the eastern coast of Italy, significant for the study of Christian architecture and art. It was a leading political center during the fifth and early sixth centuries, and some ecclesiastical architecture and artwork of that period survives, most notably the mausoleum of Galla Placidia (begun c. 425), the church of Sant' Apollinare Nuovo (begun c. 490), which is a *basilica-form church whose mosaics include both Western and later Eastern influences, and the nearby Sant' Apollinare in Classe (also a basilica; begun c. 532). Justinian made Ravenna the center of Byzantine rule in Italy, and the church of San Vitale, a centralized *church building (c. 547), is from that period. Geographically beyond the reach of the *Iconoclastic Controversy that destroyed so much art in the East, Ravenna preserves early Byzantine art to this day.

reading, reader. The public reading of biblical *lessons (readings), rooted in Jewish synagogue practice (Lk 4:17). This tradition continues in the Christian churches for *Sunday worship, *holy days and the *offices. Readings are often accompanied by *antiphons and *canticles. In many traditions both *clergy and *laity may be readers. *See also* Liturgy of the Word.

real presence. The view that Christ is present in the *Eucharist, and thus Christ, with his benefits, is conveyed to the believing *communicant. Specifically, some traditions hold that Christ's body and blood are present in the Eucharist (though differences on just what this means among various traditions can be great and of historical consequence). Some only go so far as to say that the benefits or virtues of Christ's death are communicated in the

Eucharist (virtualism), a view which maintains the Eucharist as a *means of grace. Real presence is not to be confused with *transubstantiation, which concerns the *how* of conveyance, not the *what*. Confessional statements: Aug. Conf. 10; Heid. Cat. 79; Art. Rel. 28; West. Conf. 29; CCC 1410.

rector. A head *minister or *priest.

red-letter days. In the *ABCP* those fixed *holy days of required observance, so noted because they were formerly printed in red ink. Nonrequired festal days are black-letter days.

Reformation Day (October 31). The day on which the LC and the P&RC commemorate *Luther's nailing of the *Ninety-five Theses* on the door of the Wittenberg church in 1517, considered the initial event of the Protestant Reformation.

Reformed order of worship. In the Reformed churches, an order that divides the worship service into three parts, in other words, guilt, grace and gratitude, influenced by the structure of the Heidelberg Catechism. The first part would include *confession, *absolution and the reading of the *Law (some reverse the order), the second the Scripture *readings, *sermon and *Eucharist, and the third thanksgivings and the *offering, with appropriate *hymns interspersed among the three parts. This pattern follows a kind of *ordo salutis* with response, akin to the organization of Paul's letter to the Romans.

refrigerium. In ancient Christian use, an honorary meal *with* or *for* the dead (cf. *Martyrdom of Polycarp* 18). Christians were well known for persistent *cultic observance at tombs (e.g., Monica in Augustine, *Confessions* 6), often to the dismay of the pagans (cf. Julian, *Against the Galileans* 1). Banquets are frequently represented in the art of the *catacombs of Rome, usually incorporating *fish and loaves (cf. *Didascalia Apostolorum* 6.22; *see* bread). *See also* hero cult; saints, veneration of.

regular clergy. Those *clergy in the RC who follow a *rule* (Lat. *regula*) for daily life, often situated within *monastic settings (as distinct from *secular clergy). The most famous set of clerical regulations is the *Rule of St. Benedict*.

regulative principle. The P&RC liturgical guideline (Heid. Cat. 96; West. Conf. 1.6; 21.1) that admits into worship only those components that are specifically prescribed in Scripture. Rooted in the Reformation, it differs from *Luther's perspective, which was that traditions should be maintained unless found contrary to the gospel (cf. Aug. Conf. 15).

religious. In the RC those who take *vows for Christian service in community, whether or not they have received the *sacrament of holy orders. *See* regular clergy.

reliquary. A special box or container in a church, often highly ornate, holding sacred relics.

Requiem. From Latin *requies,* "rest," a *Mass for the deceased. The sections of the *concert performance* Requiem Mass are: (1) Requiem Aeternam (Eternal Rest); (2) *Kyrie Eleison; (3) Dies Irae (The Day of Wrath); (4) Domine Jesu Christe (Lord Jesus Christ); (5) *Sanctus; (6) *Agnus Dei; (7) Lux Aeterna (Eternal Light); and (8) Libera Me (Free Me). Among the most notable musical Requiems are those by Mozart, Verdi, Fauré and Brahms (*A German Requiem*), the last nearly void of the traditional form, instead drawing its text from *Luther's translation of the Scriptures.

response. Short *acclamations or affirmations made by the *choir or *congregation in response to what the *minister has said or read. Sometimes the responses are repetitive, as during the *prayers of the people when the *congregation responds periodically, for example, "Hear our prayer."

responsive reading. An extended passage of Scripture that is read by the *minister and the *congregation in turn (note the *litany-like responses of Ps 80:2-3, 6-7, 18-19; 136; Sir 51).

responsorial psalm. Stemming from ancient practice, the *psalm recited in response to the first lesson of *Sunday worship.

Revelation, book of. A Christian canonical apocalyptic work imbued with liturgical imagery in which Christ as the slain *Lamb is the focus.

reverence. From Latin *revereor,* "to be in awe of," an aspect of biblical worship (Lev 19:30; Heb 12:28).

reverend. A title of respect given to Protestant *clergy.

revival service of worship. A type of worship service characterized by its focus on personal holiness and conversion. The revival service of worship is a recent but most influential replacement for, or modification of, the traditional liturgies of the church. It grew out of American frontier religious gatherings ("camp meetings") originally structured around the *Presbyterian sacramental seasons held four times per year as preparation for celebrating the *Eucharist (see James F. White).

There are two basic interests that influence the elements and order of the revival service. First, the focus of the preaching of the *Word is on personal holiness/betterment and ultimately the salvation of present nonbelievers, therefore making the *invitation and *altar call the goal and high point of the service rather than the *Lord's Supper, with other traditional elements such as the *Apostles' Creed, prepatory *confession and *absolution also downplayed or excluded. Second, since the climactic preaching of repentance gives direction to the service, and nonbelievers tend to be the ultimate "target audience," singing and speech-act are for the most part separated. Where the two were once intertwined throughout the long-standing liturgies, with the people responding to the unfolding drama of the liturgy, music now becomes the warm-up to the message. The focus is not on the *drama of corporate participation in the redemptive and sustaining works of God, but on the personal drama of the individual's salvation journey and climactic repentance (and thus *personal testimony* can also play a part). This revival order of service, first music and then the message, is manifest in the teaming up of Ira Sankey and Dwight Moody in the nineteenth century, and George Beverly Shea and Billy Graham in the twentieth. The revival service of worship has since influenced in various ways the order and content of many evangelical churches, an approach anticipated as early as Jonathan Edwards's joining of "sentiment" and "reason."

rite. (1) A ceremonial ritual such as baptism; (2) the *form* of a particular *liturgy. In the case of the latter, among various Christian traditions, one must distinguish between a *rite* and a *theological distinctive*. For example, the Syriac Catholic Church, an EC, is in *theological* agreement (and ecclesiastical union) with the RC, but its *rite* is more like that of the Syriac Orthodox Church, which does not hold to the christological declaration of the Council of Chalcedon (451). Table 6 maps the RC and certain EC according to *theological* similarity (rows) and *liturgical* similarity (columns).

Table 6. Theological and Liturgical Similarities in Roman Catholic and Eastern Churches

	Latin	Byzantine	W. Syrian (Antiochere)	E. Syrian (Edessene)	Coptic (Alexandrian)
Catholic →	RC		Syriac Cath. Ch. Syro-Malankara Maronite	Chaldean Cath. Ch. Syro-Malabar	
Orthodox →		Greek Orth. Russian Orth.			
Disagrees with Council → of Ephesus (431)				Assyrian Church of the East	
Disagrees with Council → of Chalcedon (451)			Syriac Orth. Ch.		Coptic Orthodox

robe. A long, flowing ecclesiastical garment rooted in antiquity, varying in *color. Ceremonially important (1) in antiquity as the white garment of the *baptized, and (2) as the distinguishing clothing of those leading the liturgy (e.g., *ministers and *choir members). The liturgical importance reaches back to OT liturgy (e.g., Ex 39:22-29) and NT liturgical imagery (Rev 6:11; 7:9). Three bars on the sleeve of a Protestant minister's *academic* robe (Geneva gown) indicate that the wearer has attained a doctor's degree.

Rogation Days. A three-day period of *supplication just before *Ascension Day (from Lat. *rogo,* "to ask"). The seasonal observance derives from ancient agricultural traditions. The *ABCP* recognizes the Monday, Tuesday and Wednesday of Holy Week as optional observances of Rogation Days, perhaps because the somber attitude of Rogation Days conflicts with the joy of *Eastertide (which includes Ascension Day).

Rogation Sunday. The fifth *Sunday after *Easter.

Roman Catholic Church. The church that recognizes the supreme authority of the *bishop of Rome (the pope). Traditionally the liturgy has been in *Latin (the official language of the RC), but since *Vatican II vernacular liturgies have been allowed around the world. A number of EC are in union with the RC (e.g., the Maronite Church), but retain their own historical *rites. The Protestant churches, which broke from Rome in the sixteenth century, retain much of the Western liturgy, regardless of theological differences. Indeed, the RC is rooted in the ancient Roman church that Paul addressed in his epistle to the Romans, and Protestant churches that retain elements of the *Roman Rite thereby enjoy a connection with the liturgy of ancient Christians. Interestingly, it is generally acknowledged that the RC has been the vanguard of the *liturgical renewal to which many Protestants find themselves drawn. *See also Apostolic Tradition;* Old Roman Creed.

Roman Rite. *Rite of the RC. Over the centuries it gradually became the dominant Western rite. Other historical Western rites are the Ambrosian (Milan), Gallican (Gaul), Mozarabic (Spain), Celtic and that of North Africa.

Romanesque church. A medieval church built in the Romanesque style, with rounded arches and vaults, heavy walls and columns, and few windows. The style is rooted in the *basilica form with influence from the Carolingian Renaissance.

rose window. A common feature of the medieval *Gothic *cathedral, a large, circular stained-glass window most often in the Western façade (the main entrance).

rubric. A guideline or instruction for carrying out a liturgy, often printed in red ink (from Lat. *ruber,* "red").

Rule of St. Benedict **(c. 540).** An influential written work laying out the duties of a *monk (i.e., *prayer, study and work).

S

Sabbath. Rooted in a Hebrew word for "rest," the Sabbath is the seventh and final day of the Jewish week (Saturday). The Sabbath begins at sunset Friday evening and ends at sunset on Saturday. This day is *holy in the Jewish religion, its proper observance being demanded in the *Ten Commandments (Ex 20:8-11). Many Christian churches have transferred the sanctity of the Sabbath to *Sunday, the primary day of Christian worship, though some Christian churches maintain keeping primary worship and rest on the Sabbath (e.g., Seventh-Day Adventists). Observance and strictures concerning the Sabbath or Sunday vary greatly among Christians, the author of the letter to the Hebrews even abstracting its meaning from calendrical observance (Heb 4:4-11; cf. Rom 14:5-6). As Saturday evening can be understood as the first part of the day of Sunday (according to OT reckoning), Sunday worship services in some churches are offered Saturday evenings.

sacrament. A visible sign (from Lat. *sacramentum;* Gk. *mystērion*) that communicates Christ's finished work, and thus is a *means of grace. The Protestant Reformers recognized only two as instituted by Jesus, *baptism and the *Eucharist, not the full seven sacraments of the RC (baptism, Eucharist, *confirmation, *penance, the *anointing of the sick, holy orders and *marriage). Not only are the sacraments central aspects of Christian worship, they are the wellspring of the Christian life. When Paul exhorts his congregations to Christian conduct, he appeals both to their baptisms (Rom 6:1-13) and their eucharistic celebrations (1 Cor 11:17-33). Confessional statements: Aug. Conf. 13; Heid. Cat. 65,

70; West. Conf. 27; CCC 1113-30. *See also* ordinance; real presence.

Sacramentary. A *liturgical book containing the various prescribed liturgical *prayers for *Masses (e.g., the *prefaces, *collects).

sacred space. A ritual sensitivity to aspects of physical space, such as the cardinal points of the compass (e.g., *church-building orientation), elevation (the *altar and *pulpit) and descent (baptismal *font), based on, for example, ancient archetypal and cultic perspectives of the heavens and the underworld.

sacred time. A liturgical sensitivity to time, both secular (as represented by the calendar) and ritual (as known in the worship service). Historian of religion Mircea Eliade (*The Sacred and the Profane*) emphasized that in sacred ritual the original (and eternal) event being celebrated is made present (sometimes referred to as *illud tempus*; cf. Rev 13:8 KJV; 22:13).

sacrifice. A frequent component of religion, especially in antiquity. There are many kinds of sacrifice, and the meanings are manifold. Specifically, sacrifice can be (1) the slaughter of a *victim*, usually an animal, at an *altar, wherein the victim may be for the satisfaction of a deity (for example, Ex 29:38-43), or for both people and the deity to share (e.g., a meal), or (2) the *offering of precious or valuable things to a deity, as, for example, Christians are to offer up sacrifices of *praise and labor to God (Heb 13:15-16; Phil 2:16-17). *See also* Paschal Lamb.

sacristy. A room set aside for storing the *Communion *wine, *bread, *chalice/cups and *paten. Also stored in the sacristy are the *robes/*vestments for the service, and therefore the room is also known as the *vestry*.

saint. From Latin *sanctus* (Gk. *hagios*, literally "holy one"), a now-deceased person officially canonized in recognition of having led a particularly godly life and/or suffered martyrdom. Held up as models (cf. *heroes; Heb 12:1: "so great a cloud of witnesses"), saints are (variably) recognized chiefly in the RC, EC, AC and LC. Certain saints, either through the presence of relics or some understood patronage, are associated with particular holy places (e.g., churches) or other institutions (e.g., hospitals, colleges). *See also* saints, veneration of.

St. Mark's, Venice. A five-domed medieval *basilica (begun in the eleventh century) informed by Byzantine architectural style, especially by the now-vanished Apostoleion in Constantinople. In the Renaissance and Baroque periods the church was the center of musical innovation under the leadership of such figures as Willaert and the *Gabrielis. Its separated choirs induced polychoral innovation, influencing the development of concertato style. The *symbol of St. Mark's is the lion.

saint, patron. A guardian *saint of a particular vocation, institution, sacred precinct, etc.

St. Paul at Jarrow. An abbey located not far from the abbey of St. Peter at Wearmouth in northern England, with which it is historically closely associated. It was founded by Benedict Biscop in 682, and *Bede spent most of his life there. The abbey was a Dark Age outpost of learning, and the Saxon period church *chancel still exists.

St. Paul's, London. The *cathedral church of London, a great *domed edifice that is the magnum opus of architect Sir Christopher *Wren (built 1675-1710).

St. Peter's, Rome. The current Renaissance and Baroque *cathedral on the Vatican Hill, whose construction under Pope Julius II (beg. 1506) replaced Constantine's *Old St. Peter's. It is the seat of the *bishop of Rome (the pope). The cathedral was designed by Donato Bramante and Carlo Maderno, and its great *dome by Michelangelo. Archaeologically, the main *altar, with a grand *baldachino by Bernini, sits atop a vertical succession of altars reaching down to a second-century memorial (*aedicula*) to Peter. This memorial is within a mostly pagan necropolis discovered in the mid-twentieth century, among whose tombs is that of the Julii, with its oldest known Christian mosaic (motifs include Christ as Helios with chariot, and *Jonah and the sea creature).

St.-Denis. The royal *abbey outside of Paris. It was the font of *Gothic church architecture under the leadership of the *abbot Suger, its pointed arches and ribbed vaulting becoming standard.

Sainte-Marie-Madeleine, Vézelay. A French *Romanesque *abbey church (built early twelfth century). A popular destination for pilgrims, it is known, among other things, for its relief sculpture of the Mission of the Apostles in the *tympanum above the central portal, as well as for other tympana reliefs.

saints, veneration of. The honoring and invoking of particular saints for their holiness and intercession before God. By the middle of the second century Christian martyrs were venerated with annual honors, as suggested by the case of Polycarp (martyred 155). In the eighteenth chapter of *The Martyrdom of Polycarp* it is said that on the anniversary of his death (his *dies natalis* in Christian parlance) he was to receive annual honors at his tomb. Despite voices to the contrary, such *cult is to some extent likely rooted in pagan *hero cult (substituting "martyr" or "saint" for "hero"), where annual *feasting on the anniversary of the death of a hero was customary, as were honors at the tomb, as Augustine's mother Monica was inclined to give (*Confessions* 6.2). The association was also made in the area of architecture as the tombs and memorials (*martyria*) of the martyrs and *saints utilized heroic architectural funerary forms (e.g., circular and *octagonal structures) and concepts (e.g., relics). *See also* Church of the Holy Sepulchre; Sanctoral.

salutation. The *minister's greeting in which the minister says (e.g.) "The Lord be with you," and the people respond, "And also with you" (cf. 2 Tim 4:22). The *collect often immediately follows.

Sanctoral. A *liturgical book containing the calendar and service-particulars for the feast days of *saints and martyrs.

sanctuary. In Protestant churches the location of regular Christian corporate worship. It is *sanctus*, set apart for *holy purposes. (In the RC, when crossing the *threshold to enter the place of worship, worshipers sprinkle themselves with holy water.) In the RC and the OC, *sanctuary* refers not to the *nave (where the *laity are) but the area where the *altar, *apse and *officiants are located, functioning in the OC as a "holy of holies." The special status of the sanctuary is particularly applicable during the worship service itself, since the sanctuary is the location where God meets the people, the meeting place of heaven and earth. Indeed, in the Syrian churches the sanctuary with its liturgy is identified with heaven. *See also* heavenly liturgy.

Sanctus. A Latin word meaning *holy, the Sanctus is part of the *Ordinary of the Latin *Mass, well known for the thrice-repeated "Holy, holy, holy" (Is 6:3; Rev 4:8; in Latin called the *Ter Sanctus*) in which the earthly *congregation joins the heavenly host in the *heavenly liturgy. It is part of the *Liturgy of the Eucharist, often followed by the *Benedictus Qui Venit (Mt 21:9). Its place in the liturgy is quite early in date (Cyr., *Myst. Cat.* 5.6; cf. *1 Clem.* 34.6-7). It is not to be confused with the hymn "Holy, Holy, Holy!" by Reginald Heber (1826).

Santiago de Compostela. A *Romanesque *cathedral in northern Spain that was a popular destination for medieval *pilgrimages. The church is named after St. *James (= *Santiago*).

sarcophagus. From Greek for "flesh-eater," a carved stone coffin utilized by the well-to-do in the ancient world. Many important illustrations and *symbols are found on Christian sarcophagi dating as early as the third century, including *Jonah and the sea creature, the *baptism of Jesus and the miracle of the loaves.

Sarum Rite. Associated with the diocese of Salisbury (both Old and New Sarum), a dominant *rite in England when the Reformation began. It provided elements *Cranmer used in reordering the *Daily Office in the *BCP*.

Scripture reading. *See* reading, reader.

sealing. In Greek *sphragizō*, "to seal," a ritual anointing with *oil (*see also* chrism) that secures the believer as God's own, the *sign of the cross being frequently made with the oil. Associated with *baptism (2 Cor 1:21-22; Eph 1:13-14), it is mainly *symbolic of the Holy Spirit's work in salvation (Eph 4:30). In early Syrian Christianity anointing with oil emphasized birth as the chief aspect of baptism, rather than dying and rising. *See also* chrismation; confirmation.

season. Any extended liturgical period of observance: *Advent, *Christmas, *Epiphany, *Lent, *Easter and *Pentecost. *See* liturgical year.

secular clergy. In the RC those *priests who live and work outside of a *monastic setting or order, in the everyday world of the *laity (e.g., parish priests).

seeker service. Rooted in the evangelistic goals of the *revival service of worship, a worship service sensitive to, or geared for, the felt-needs, apprehensions and cultural preferences of seekers (i.e., non-Christians in attendance). Examples of such accommodation may include *praise music rather than traditional *hymnody, theater seating in the *sanctuary, coffee during the service and an optional Saturday evening service. The *sermon tends to stress issues of personal, daily application.

selah. Hebrew word meaning "pause," "reflect" or perhaps "bow." Found in a number of the *psalms.

Septuagesima. Latin for "seventieth," the third *Sunday before the beginning of *Lent.

Septuagint. The Greek translation of the Hebrew Bible (OT) made in the third and second centuries B.C., mostly at Alexandria, Egypt. It is abbreviated LXX due to the tradition that seventy (or seventy-two) scholars participated in the translation. It was the Bible of the synagogue of the Jewish diaspora in the Hellenistic/Roman world. It was frequently the version of the OT cited by the authors of the NT, exhibiting important variants from the Hebrew text of the OT, and thus it has additional importance to modern biblical studies. It contains a number of Jewish books not found in the Hebrew Bible (*see* Apocrypha). It is the preferred version of the OT in the Greek Orthodox Church. *Codex Vaticanus contains much of the Septuagint.

sequence. During the Middle Ages, texts set to the musical embellishments of the *Alleluias, but later becoming independent texts inserted into a fixed liturgy, especially on festal occasions.

sermon. In the worship service, the elucidation or exegesis given by the presiding *minister concerning any of the readings. Uncommon in the EC, it is of great importance in Protestant churches, as Protestants since *Zwingli have elevated the preaching of the *Word to prominence in the worship service.

service. *See* liturgy.

service of light. An ancient evening *rite (cf. *Ap. Trad.* 29C) associated with *Vespers, also called the *Lucernarium.* It is probably a Christian parallel to the pre-Christian greeting of the lamp at night, the light now *symbolic of Christ (Jn 8:12). The *Phos Hilaron is sung during this service. A number of Protestant service books now include an evening service of light.

Sexagesima. Latin for "sixtieth," the second *Sunday before the beginning of *Lent.

Shepherd of Hermas. A Roman treatise written over a period of time between 100 and 135. Sometimes described as an apocalypse, it was used in ancient Christian *congregations, even (partially) included with the NT books in Codex Sinaiticus.

sign of the cross. The *gesture of making a *cross over one's forehead and/or upper torso, and that *officiants make over people and sacred objects. Given initially as part of *sealing at *baptism, in worship the gesture honors the Son and/or the Holy Trinity, and also brings to memory one's own baptism and the sealing of the Holy Spirit. Some think of it as warding off evil (e.g., *Ap. Trad.* 42), perhaps based on Revelation 7:3, 4; 9:4.

silence. An attitude of or moment for preparation, *reverence and reflection.

singing. *See* music.

solemnity. In the RC, the highest ranking *holy days.

solstice. A solar phenomenon held as significant since at least Neolithic times (e.g., Stonehenge) wherein the sun reaches the annual extremities of its latitudinal movement. The *winter solstice* (in the Northern Hemisphere) takes place on December 21/22, and is the shortest day of the year (i.e., the least amount of sunlight, the longest night). Such an occasion anticipates the gradual increase of daylight and thus is often associated with a *new year. The *summer solstice* occurs on June 20/21 and is the day of greatest sunlight. *See also* Blue Christmas.

Song of Mary. *See* Magnificat.

Song of Moses (Cantemus Domino). Moses' song after the defeat of the Egyptian army at the Red Sea (Ex 15:1-18). Appropriate during *Eastertide, it is not to be confused with the Song of Moses at Deuteronomy 32:1-43.

Song of Simeon. *See* Nunc Dimittis.

Song of the Redeemed. *See* Magna et Mirabilia.

Song of the Three Jews. A book in the *Apocrypha also known as Song of the Three Children, which in the *Septuagint is an addition to the third chapter of the book of Daniel. The song includes (1) the Benedictus Es, Domine, a *canticle beginning "Blessed are you, O Lord," based on Song of the Three 1:29-34 (NRSV; Dan 3:52-56 in the LXX and others), and (2) the Benedicite, Omnia Opera Domini, a canticle beginning "Bless the Lord, all you works of the Lord," based on Song of the Three 1:35-65 (NRSV; Dan 3:57-87 in the LXX and others). These three children are found visually portrayed in the Christian *catacombs, perhaps symbolic of faithful endurance in times of persecution.

Song of Zechariah (Benedictus Dominus Deus). A song beginning "Blessed be the Lord God of Israel" (Lk 1:68-79), one of three Gospel *canticles found in the first two chapters of Luke. Appropriate at *Morning Prayer.

Songs of Isaiah. In the *EBCP*, texts from the book of Isaiah recited as *canticles: Isaiah 12:2-6 (Ecce, Deus), Isaiah 55:6-11 (Quaerite Dominum) and portions of Isaiah 60:1-19 (Surge, Illuminare).

Sovik, Edward (b. 1918). An American church architect who, in his book *Architecture for Worship* (1973), downplays a church interior divided into *nave and *chancel sections, emphasizing instead that the worship space be a comfortable, multipurpose *centrum* for the gathering of the Christian community, a "shelter for *people*" rather than a "House of God."

sponsor. A church member or other *baptized Christian who vouches for the life and conduct of a baptismal candidate. *See* godparent.

spontaneous worship. An unplanned aspect of a worship service that arises at the moment, from improvised elements of corporate *prayer to (perhaps) manifestations of the *charismata (cf. 1 Cor 14:26). Such spontaneity is usually regulated by the traditional *form of the service (cf. 1 Cor 14:40). Moments of spontaneity often allow freer participation of the *laity in corporate worship (e.g., impromptu *acclamations). In *Pentecostal worship, where spontaneity is highly valued, lay participation is strong.

standing. A gesture of respect and honor, often made during the singing of *hymns and the *Gospel reading. In the OC it is traditional for the congregation to stand most if not all of the service, as was the custom in the ancient church (pews emerged in the Middle Ages).

Stations of the Cross (*Via Crucis*). A liturgical drama of the final hours of Jesus' *Passion. Table 7 presents the traditional stations and those of Pope John Paul II (based solely on the *Gospel narratives).

steeple. A towerlike church architectural feature. The steeple rose to prominence due to the architectural influence of Christopher *Wren. It is a feature of New England churches, though it can be found throughout the United States.

Stephen, Feast of (December 26). An ancient commemoration of Stephen, the *deacon who was the church's first martyr (Acts 7:58). It coincides with Boxing Day in certain Commonwealth countries, a day of giving to the poor.

Table 7. Stations of the Cross

Traditional Stations	Stations of Pope John Paul II
Jesus is condemned to death	Jesus in the garden of Gethsemane
Jesus receives the cross	Jesus, betrayed by Judas, is arrested
Jesus falls the first time	
Jesus is met by his blessed mother	Jesus is condemned by the Sanhedrin
Simon of Cyrene helps Jesus to carry his cross	Jesus is denied by Peter
Veronica wipes the face of Jesus	Jesus is judged by Pilate
Jesus falls the second time	Jesus is scourged and crowned with thorns
The women of Jerusalem mourn for our Lord	Jesus bears the cross
Jesus falls for the third time	Jesus is helped by Simon the Cyrenian to carry the cross
Jesus is stripped of his garments	Jesus meets the women of Jerusalem
Jesus is nailed to the cross	Jesus is crucified
Jesus dies on the cross	Jesus promises his kingdom to the good thief
Jesus is taken down from the cross	Jesus speaks to his mother and the disciple
Jesus is placed in the tomb	Jesus dies on the cross
	Jesus is placed in the tomb

stole. A sacred *vestment comprised of a band of cloth worn around the neck and down the front of the priest or minister, an authoritative vestment of *ordination. Its *color usually corresponds to the appropriate liturgical color.

strophic. A song's stanzas all sung to the same melody. If a refrain separates the verses, then the form is verse-chorus-verse.

suffrages. Prayerful *petitions.

Sunday. The first day of the week. In the history of the Christian church, every Sunday is a *feast of Jesus Christ, his Sunday resurrection (Jn 20:1) celebrated weekly. As such it is a day of joy. Evidence for corporate worship is found as early as the NT and *Apostolic Fathers (1 Cor 16:2; Acts 20:7; Rev 1:10; *Did.* 14.1; Ign., *Magn.* 9.1; Just., *1 Apol.* 67.3).

sunrise. *See* east.

supplication. A humble *petitioning.

surplice. *See* alb.

Sursum Corda. Latin for "Lift up your hearts," the first part of the *Liturgy of the Eucharist, opening with the lines "The Lord be with you. / And also with you." It is an ancient part of Christian liturgy that is at least as old as the *Apostolic Tradition* (4.3; also Cyr., *Myst. Cat.* 5.4).

symbol. Something presented to the senses that evokes a more complex reality. The liturgy is replete with symbols, including not only simple visual representations (*see* iconography) and *gestures, but also elements of *sacred space and *sacred time. For the ancient church Clement of Alexandria listed a number of valid visual symbols (*Christ the Educator* 3.11), including the *dove, the *fish and the anchor. *See also* catacombs, Christian Roman.

synaxis. An assembly, specifically a gathering for corporate worship (cognate to *synagogue*). According to some, in the ancient church the synaxis was a separate service occurring before the *eucharistic service (i.e., the *Liturgy of the Word), though others today would appear to apply the term to the *Liturgy of the Eucharist as well.

Syria. One of the earliest bases of nascent Christianity, Antioch in particular of great importance (Acts 11:26; 13:1; cf. Gal 2:11-12). Syria was a center for the production of ancient *Gospels (especially Matthew; perhaps Luke and John, as well as apocryphal Gospels). The Syrian tradition preserved the Semitic character of ancient Christianity. Its Christian *rites influenced churches of other geographical areas. The earliest extant *church building has been uncovered near the Euphrates in eastern Syria (*see* Dura-Europos, church building of). An area of creative and reflective energy, it was perhaps the provenance of certain Gnostic beliefs. Significant writers from Syria include *Ephrem and Theodore of Mopsuestia, and significant liturgical writings include the *Didache*, the *Didascalia* and the *Apostolic Constitutions*. *See also* Syriac.

Syriac. A language of the ancient *Syrian church that is a later dialect of Aramaic, the language Jesus spoke.

T

tabernacle. (1) In the OT, the original, portable "house" for God during the wilderness wanderings up until the time of Solomon; (2) in the RC the *baldachino over the *altar of a church; (3) the baldachino-like container for the post-eucharistic *host, accessible as a place of adoration and *prayer within the *church building.

Table of the Lord. An expression used by Paul for the *Eucharist (1 Cor 10:21). "Table" in antiquity (Gk. *trapeza*; Lat. *mensa*) can communicate a ritual/*sacrificial sense, as pagan inscriptions in Greek mention the cultic "table of the god" (see Gill); one *shares* (*see koinōnia*) in table fellowship that often includes the deity (in Gk., *trapeza* can also refer to the sacrifice itself). Paul's "table" would seem to imply something along this line (1 Cor 10:18-20), where the Israelite *altar (Gk. *thusiastērion*, literally "place for sacrifice"; cf. Ezek 41:22; Mal 1:7, 12) and pagan sacrificial table for the deity (Gk. *trapeza*) are paralleled with the Table of the Lord (cf. Germ. 4). However, many within the P&RC have understood "table" to mean dining furniture, and have utilized a wooden table with chairs rather than the traditional altar for the place of *Communion, or even have chosen to take Communion in the pews. Some Christian *catacomb tombs were equipped with a *mensa*, though most likely for the purpose of a *refrigerium*.

Taizé. A Protestant-founded *monastic community in France formed in the mid-twentieth century having an ecumenical emphasis. Its music is highly appreciated, and the community is a popular place for visitors, especially youth.

Te Deum [Laudamus]. Latin for "[We Praise] You, God," an ancient *hymn of the church, appropriate in the *Morning Office. A famous setting is by Anton Bruckner.

temple. *See* sanctuary.

Ten Commandments. Also known as the Decalogue (literally "ten words" or "ten statements"), the list of commandments found at Exodus 20:1-17 (also Deut 5:6-21). Enumeration differs between most Protestants on the one hand, and the LC and RC on the other, the numbering of the prohibition of images (Ex 20:4) being the crux of the difference.

Tenebrae. Latin meaning "darkness," historically in the RC the morning *offices prayed on *Maundy Thursday, *Good Friday and *Holy Saturday, marked by candle-extinguishing, an aspect that is retained even among Protestants today in their Tenebrae services on Maundy Thursday and Good Friday.

Tertullian (fl. c. turn of the third century). A North African Christian theologian who wrote (in Latin), among other things, on the liturgy, including the important *De baptismo*. His work on the doctrine of the Holy *Trinity was influential.

Thanksgiving. The *prayer that follows the *Sursum Corda in the *Liturgy of the Eucharist (Cyr., *Myst. Cat.* 5.5), opening with the *Vere dignum* ("It is meet and right"). The ancient *Apostolic Tradition* (4.4-10) divides its Thanksgiving into four parts: for the *creation, the incarnation, Jesus' suffering and death, and the Eucharist (cf. Justin, *Dial.* 41; see Dix [B]).

Thanksgiving Day. In the United States a harvest celebration with its source in the Plymouth, Massachusetts, colony (1621). It was officially established as a national holiday by President Abraham Lincoln (1863) and set to its present observance on the fourth Thursday of November by President Franklin D. Roosevelt (adopted 1941). Canadian Thanksgiving is the second Monday in October.

Thanksgiving, Great. *See* Eucharistic Prayer.

"This is the feast of victory." The *antiphon to the hymn "Worthy Is Christ" (by John W. Arthur, based on texts from Revelation). It is especially sung in American LC as part of the *Liturgy of the Word (as an alternative to the *Gloria in Excelsis Deo), every *Sunday being a *feast of Jesus Christ.

Thomas, Feast of (December 21). A celebration of the "doubting" apostle Thomas, an enigmatic figure of ancient Christianity. Syrian Christians knew him as Judas Thomas, *Thomas* being Aramaic for "twin" (*Didymus* is the Greek form of *Thomas:* Jn 20:24). Since likely a twin, early speculation thought him a twin of Jesus (*Book of Thomas the Contender* 138; *Acts of Thomas* 39). The OC recognizes the first *Sunday after *Easter as Thomas Sunday (cf. Acts 5:12-20; Jn 20:19-31). An optional feast date in the WC is July 3.

threshold. The point where a person leaves one room or spatial environment and enters another. In the ancient world it was significant (Homer, *Odyssey* 7.82-3; Apuleius, *Metamorphoses* 11.23) as thresholds delineated *sacred space. For example, the threshold of the entrance of a residence, covered with the blood of the *Paschal Lamb, designated the sphere of God's protection in Egypt (Ex 12:7, 13). The *Dura-Europos church building had symbolic lettering inscribed on or near various doorways (see Kraeling). In the RC a person sprinkles with holy water when entering the *nave (cf. Vergil, *Aeneid* 6.635-6).

thurible. *See* censer.

thurifer. The person who carries the *censer in the *procession.

tithe. Meaning "tenth," the amount demanded of one's increase in the OT (Deut 14:22-23). Now it is often synonymous with *offering*.

titulus. The name given to property that early Christians were granted (i.e., *titled*) for churches in ancient Rome (at least as early as the fourth century). These important ancient establishments, usually associated with residential structures, include S. Clemente and SS. Giovanni e Paolo.

transept. In church architecture, the area of a *basilica or *cathedral that runs perpendicularly across the *nave, bisecting the church into nave and *choir/*sanctuary sections. See the appendix.

Transfiguration, Feast of the (August 6). A day commemorating Jesus' remarkable transfiguration before three of his disciples (Mt 17:1-8 par.). Like the *baptism of Jesus, Jesus' *glory and divine sonship were manifested in a special way. The *Revised Common *Lectionary* celebrates this feast the *Sunday preceding *Ash Wednesday (i.e., around the end of *Christmas/*Epiphany season; certain themes are common to Christmas, Epiphany and the transfiguration).

transubstantiation. The belief that the *bread and *wine of *Communion become, *substantially*, the body and blood of Jesus during the *Eucharistic Prayer (CCC 1376). In the RC this occurs with the *Words of Institution; in the EC it occurs with the *Epiclesis, the work of the Holy Spirit akin to the incarnation event (cf. John of Damascus, *Orthodox Faith* 4.13). Protestants deny the *change* of substance.

trefoil. From Latin *trifolium*, "three-leaved" (e.g., a clover), a symbol of the *Trinity.

Tridentine Rite. The *rite sanctioned by the RC at the Council of Trent (1545-1563).

triduum. The time period beginning the evening of *Maundy Thursday and ending the evening of *Easter Sunday, which period constitutes the high point of the Christian *liturgical year.

trine immersion. The practice by some Christian groups to immerse the initiate three times during the *rite of *baptism, each immersion corresponding to a person of the *Trinity (Mt 28:19). Trine immersion is quite ancient (*Ap. Trad.* 21.14; Cyr., *Myst. Cat.* 2.4; cf. *Did.* 7.3) and still practiced quite often among the EC. Other groups today embracing this *rite include the Amish, Mennonites, Brethren in Christ and Grace Brethren.

Trinity Sunday. A major feast, the eighth *Sunday after *Easter. The *Athanasian Creed is recited in many Protestant churches on this day. In the OC, Trinity Sunday is the seventh Sunday after Easter, and thus equates to the Day of *Pentecost. Color: white.

Trinity, the Holy. The Father, the Son and the Holy Spirit, the recognition and evocation of whom is an ancient part of Christian liturgy (e.g., Mt 28:19).

Triodion. The OC season and corresponding liturgical text covering the period beginning the Sunday of the Publican and Pharisee (i.e., the fourth Sunday before *Lent) through *Holy Saturday.

triptych. From Greek *triptychos*, "threefold," a three-paneled altarpiece. Famous painters of triptychs include Jan van *Eyck and Hieronymus Bosch. A screen or panel placed behind an *altar is called a reredos.

Trisagion. From Greek meaning "three times holy" (cf. Is 6:3), a *hymn sung especially in EC liturgies. *See also* Sanctus.

troparion. A brief *hymn; hymnic response or refrain. *See also* strophic.

trope. A textual embellishment of a fixed liturgical text, such as the four *Christmas texts added to *Bach's *Magnificat in E-flat major.

tune name. The title given to a musical composition to which a *hymn of appropriate meter is matched.

Twenty-third Psalm. Also called the Shepherd's Psalm (Psalm 22 in the LXX). In the ancient church the baptismal initiates sang this *psalm during the initiatory *rites, such as *baptism (vv. 2, 4), *sealing (v. 5) and first *Communion (v. 5), Christ the *Good

Shepherd (v. 1) with them all along (e.g., Cyr., *Myst. Cat.* 4.7; see Danielou). Often associated with *funerary rites, it is recited on All Souls' Day (*see* All Saints' Day).

tympanum. In medieval church architecture, a relief sculpture in a semicircular space over a doorway, often featuring Jesus at the center. It maintains the *apsidal *dome of heaven motif, and thus may incorporate the symbols of the zodiac (cf. the more ancient Mithraic *tauroctony*).

type, biblical. An OT event, object, *symbol or *rite that is understood as anticipating or elucidating a NT event or rite (e.g., 1 Pet 3:20-21). Consequently *lessons from the OT are often selected to complement the NT lessons. *See analogia fidei.*

U

unity. The desire of Jesus Christ for his people (Jn 17:11), expressed in the *Eucharist (1 Cor 11:18-21, 33). In light of this, gathered Christians sing in unison and corporately recite *prayers and *creeds (cf. Rom 15:5-6). *See also* agape.

V

Vatican II. A groundbreaking RC council (1962-1965). It included, among other things, important directives for *liturgical renewal, such as those found in the conciliar documents *Sacrosanctum concilium* and *Lumen Gentium*. The council is also acknowledged as a major influence on Protestant liturgical renewal.

Venite. Latin meaning "O, Come," the name of Psalm 95. Assigned to *Morning Prayer, even today it is a popular text drawn on for *contemporary worship.

versicle, verse. A short statement (and sometimes ensuing *response) taken from Scripture.

Vespers. In the *Daily Office, the *office at evening (from Gk. *hesperos*, "evening star," i.e., Venus). In the AC it is known as Evensong. Traditionally the service includes the Gospel *canticle *Magnificat. For general form *see* Daily Office. *See also* Evening Prayer.

vessels. The containers for the celebration of the *Eucharist, such as the *cruet, *paten and *chalice.

vestments. Liturgical attire worn by the *clergy, *choir and *lay assistants in the worship service (e.g., *robes).

vestry. A room in a church serving the same purpose as a *sacristy. In the AC a *vestry* is also a committee of *lay people who oversee the mundane operations of a church (and thus *vestryman*).

Viaticum. The meal "for the journey," the final *Eucharist administered to the dying as part of "Last Rites."

vigil. A watch throughout the hours of the *night. The Saturday evening vigil (a *liturgical drama) is ancient, though more frequent in the EC, whose texts were set to music in a well-known work by Rachmaninov (1915).

vine. The plant that produces the grape, associated with *wine, and the basis for Jesus' referring to himself as the "True Vine" (Jn 15:1). Frequently found depicted in ancient funerary settings, it evokes a sense of paradisiacal life and repose.

virgin. An *ascetic ideal connected with purity and devotion (cf. 2 Cor 11:2; Rev 14:4), even being set apart (i.e., *holy*) for service to a deity. A Christian virgin (Gk. *parthenos*; Lat. *virgo*) devoted to the service of God is as early as the NT, both in the case of the Virgin *Mary and *Philip the evangelist's four virgin daughters who prophesy (Acts 21:9; cf. *Ap. Trad.* 12; though note 1 Cor 7:25-28, 37-38).

Visitation, Feast of the (May 31). *See* Mary, the Virgin.

visitors. Worship service attendees who are neither *baptized members nor *catechumens. Traditionally excluded from attending the *Liturgy of the Eucharist, such strictures are now quite relaxed. Christians are encouraged to demonstrate the ancient value of hospitality (Gk. *philoxenia*) toward strangers and unbelievers (Heb 13:2).

vow. A solemn pledge taken by *religious orders. Standard are those of poverty, chastity and obedience.

Vulgate. A Latin translation of the Bible prepared mostly by Jerome, and historically the Bible of the RC.

W

Washington National Cathedral. Begun in 1907 and completed in 1990, the *Episcopal Cathedral Church of Saint Peter and Saint

Paul located in Washington, D.C. It has been used for certain United States national religious services (e.g., presidential funerals; a 9/11 memorial).

water. A symbol of life and purification, the visible element of *baptism. In the biblical literature it is closely associated with divine acts of creation, judgment and deliverance (Gen 1; 7; Ex 14; Josh 3; 1 Pet 3:20-21).

Watts, Isaac (1674-1748). An English Independent hymnist who composed original lyrics often set to preexisting metrical *hymn tunes. Representative hymns: "Our God, Our Help in Ages Past," "When I Survey the Wondrous Cross."

Wesley, Charles (1707-1788). An English hymnist with thousands of hymns to his credit, and brother of John Wesley, the founder of Methodism. Some of his lyrics anticipate the *gospel song of first-person emphasis. Though his hymns are personal in expression, they retain theological integrity. He composed with the *liturgical year in mind. Representative hymns: "Blessed Be the Name," "Christ the Lord Is Risen Today," "Hark! The Herald Angels Sing" (now often set to music by Felix Mendelssohn), "Jesus, Lover of My Soul," "O for a Thousand Tongues to Sing."

west. In antiquity, the direction of sunset and thus the underworld and its dead (cf. the journey of Odysseus). In ancient Egypt, royalty were buried on the western side of the Nile, the deceased pharaoh identified with Osiris, the "lord of the west," ruler of the dead. Early Christian *basilicas with funerary connotations, such as *Old St. Peter's, were orientated toward the west. In the ancient church the baptismal initiate was to face west to renounce the devil and all his works (Cyr., *Myst. Cat.* 1.2, 4).

Westminster Confession of Faith (1646). The *confession of faith agreed on by a large committee of *Presbyterians, *Anglicans and Independents, and authorized by the British Parliament (thus the reference to *Westminster*). Strongly Calvinistic, it is an official statement of faith of Presbyterian churches. It has also, with modifications, been accepted by certain Baptists. Companion documents include the Shorter and Larger Catechisms.

Whitsunday. The seventh *Sunday after *Easter and closely associated or synonymous with *Pentecost.

wine. A symbol of life and vitality in the ancient world and the ritual sign of Jesus' blood in the *Eucharist.

Word of God, the. The *holy Scriptures as embraced by the church, the *Old and *New Testaments. The Word of God is the textual center of Christian liturgies. *See also* Apocrypha; Gospel(s); Liturgy of the Word; Psalter.

Words of Institution. In the *Eucharistic Prayer, the minister's speech-act of reciting Jesus' words at the *Last Supper (Mk 14:22-24: "Take; this is my body. . . . This is my blood . . ."). These words are usually acknowledged as a necessary element of the *Communion service. In the RC *transubstantiation occurs when the Words of Institution are spoken (CCC 1354; cf. Iren., *Haer.* 4.17.5). *See also* Epiclesis.

worship. From older English *worthship*, reverence rendered to God. Gathered believers are now the temple of God (1 Cor 3:16—*you* is pl.), and are to worship in truth (Jn 4:23-24), sincerity (Mt 15:8-9) and *reverence (Is 6:1-3; Lk 18:9-14), "decently and in order" (1 Cor 14:40). *Liturgy provides the framework for worship. The content of ancient Christian worship is found at Acts 2:42: the apostles' teaching, *Communion and *prayer—the rudiments of the *Liturgy of the Word, the *Liturgy of the Eucharist and the *Daily Office. Corporate worship is enjoined at Hebrews 10:25, and Christ promises his presence when two or more are gathered (Mt 18:20). Weekly worship is noted as early as Acts (20:7; cf. 1 Cor 16:2) and Justin Martyr (*1 Apol.* 66).

worship leader. The person who directs the music portion of a *contemporary worship service, as worship has more and more become synonymous with musical *praise.

worship team. Also known as a praise team, an ensemble for leading corporate singing in *contemporary worship services. Its innovation is recent (c. 1980s). It is usually comprised of rock-band instrumentalists (who play, e.g., electric guitars, keyboards and drums) and lead singers who face the congregation in concert style. The use of a worship team in traditional and liturgical services is a growing phenomenon (*see* convergence service).

Wren, Sir Christopher (1632-1723). The British architect who oversaw the design of more than fifty *church buildings, including *St. Paul's, London. He preferred open church interiors, doing away with the *chancel screen (opting for the *Communion *rail) and taking into consideration the auditory needs of the congregation.

X, Y, Z

Zwingli, Ulrich (1484-1531). The most important leader of the nascent Swiss Reformation, whose *symbolic understanding of the Eucharist (i.e., "this is my body" is figurative) has echoed throughout sections of Protestantism. Other areas in which he influenced the P&RC include quarterly Communion and a high value placed on teaching the *Word of God.

Appendix

Basic floor plan of a basilica-form church

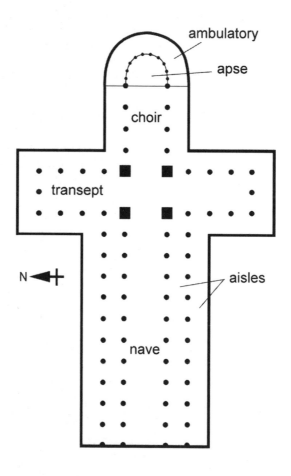

Drawing by Mitchell Provance.

Bibliography

In addition to the works listed below, general works particularly helpful to research for this dictionary included Peter E. Fink, *The New Dictionary of Sacramental Worship*; Angelo Di Berardino, *Encyclopedia of the Early Church*; F. L. Cross and E. A. Livingstone, *The Oxford Dictionary of the Christian Church*; and Michael Kennedy, *The Oxford Dictionary of Music*.

Adam, Adolf. *The Liturgical Year: Its History and Meaning After the Reform of the Liturgy*. Translated by Matthew J. O'Connell. Collegeville, Minn.: Liturgical Press, 1990.

Baltzer, Klaus. *Deutero-Isaiah: A Commentary on Isaiah 40-55*. Edited by Peter Machinist. Translated by Margaret Kohl. Hermeneia. Minneapolis, Minn.: Fortress Press, 2001.

Baumstark, Anton. *Comparative Liturgy*. Revised by Bernard Botte. Translated by F. L. Cross. Westminster, Md.: Newman Press, 1958.

Book of Common Prayer and Administration of the Sacraments and Other Rites and Ceremonies of the Church, Together with The Psalter or Psalms of David, According to the Use of The Episcopal Church, The. New York: Seabury Press, 1979.

Bradshaw, Paul F. [A] *The Search for the Origins of Christian Worship: Sources and Methods for the Study of Early Liturgy*. New York: Oxford University Press, 1992.

―――. [B] *Two Ways of Praying*. Nashville: Abingdon, 1995.

―――. [C] *Eucharistic Origins*. Oxford: Oxford University Press, 2004.

Bradshaw, Paul F., Maxwell E. Johnson and L. Edward Phillips. Edited by Harold W. Attridge. *The Apostolic Tradition: A Commentary*. Hermeneia. Minneapolis, Minn.: Fortress Press, 2002.

Burkert, Walter. *Ancient Mystery Cults*. Carl Newell Jackson Lectures. Cambridge, Mass.: Harvard University Press, 1987.

Carpenter, Delores, general ed. Nolan E. Williams Jr., music ed. *African American Heritage Hymnal*. Chicago, Ill.: GIA Publications, 2001.

Carrington, Philip. *The Primitive Christian Calendar: A Study in the Making of the Marcan Gospel*. Vol. 1. Introduction and Text. Cambridge: Cambridge University Press, 1952.

Cyril of Jerusalem. *St. Cyril of Jerusalem's Lectures on the Christian Sacraments: The Procatechesis and the Five Mystagogical Catecheses.* Edited by F. L. Cross. Crestwood, N.Y.: St. Vladimir's Seminary Press, 1995.

Danielou, Jean. *The Bible and the Liturgy.* Ann Arbor, Mich.: Servant Books, 1979.

Dix, Dom Gregory. [A] *The Shape of the Liturgy.* London: Dacre Press, 1945.

————, ed. [B] *The Treatise on the Apostolic Tradition of St. Hippolytus of Rome, Bishop and Martyr.* 2nd ed. Reissued with corrections, preface and bibliography by Henry Chadwick. London: Society for Promoting Christian Knowledge, 1968.

Germanus of Constantinople. *On the Divine Liturgy.* The Greek text with translation, introduction and commentary by Paul Meyendorff. Crestwood, N.Y.: St. Vladimir's Seminary Press, 1999.

Gill, David. "*Trapezomata:* A Neglected Aspect of Greek Sacrifice." *Harvard Theological Review* 67 (1974): 117-37.

Grabar, André. "Christian Architecture, East & West." *Archaeology* 2 (1949): 95-104.

Hammond, Peter. *Liturgy and Architecture.* New York: Columbia University Press, 1961.

Horbury, William. *Herodian Judaism and New Testament Study.* Wissenschaftliche Untersuchungen zum Neuen Testament 193. Tübingen: Mohr Siebeck, 2006.

Kelly, J. N. D. *Early Christian Creeds.* 2nd ed. London: Longmans, 1960.

Keyte, Hugh, and Andrew Parrott, eds. Clifford Bartlett, assoc. ed. *The New Oxford Book of Carols.* Oxford: Oxford University Press, 1992.

Kraeling, Carl H., with a contribution by C. Bradford Welles. *The Christian Building.* Yale University Excavations at Dura-Europos. Final Report, vol. 8, part 2. New Haven, Conn.: Dura-Europos Publications; Locust Valley, N.Y.: distributed by J. J. Augustin, 1967.

Krautheimer, Richard. *Early Christian and Byzantine Architecture.* 4th ed. Revised by Richard Krautheimer and Slobodan Ćurčić. New Haven, Conn.: Yale University Press, 1986.

Laager, Jacques. "Epiklesis." In *Reallexikon für Antike und Christen-*

tum: Sachwörterbuch zur Auseinandersetzung des Christentums mit der antiken Welt, 5:578-99. Edited by Theodore Klauser. Stuttgart, Germany: A. Hiersemann, 1962.

Lehmann, Karl. "The Dome of Heaven." *Art Bulletin* 27 (1945): 1-27.

LeMarquand, Grant. "The Anglican Church of Kenya." In *The Oxford Guide to The Book of Common Prayer: A Worldwide Survey*, edited by Charles Hefling and Cynthia Shattuck, pp. 287-97. New York: Oxford University Press, 2006.

Levenson, Jon D. *The Death and Resurrection of the Beloved Son: The Transformation of Child Sacrifice in Judaism and Christianity*. New Haven, Conn.: Yale University Press, 1993.

Malina, Bruce J. *On the Genre and Message of Revelation: Star Visions and Sky Journeys*. Peabody, Mass.: Hendrickson, 1995.

Osten-Sacken, Peter von der. "Christologie, Taufe, Homologie— Ein Beitrag zu Apc Joh 1 5f." *Zeitschrift für die neutestamentliche Wissenschaft und die Kunde der älteren Kirche* 58 (1967): 255-66.

Riley, Gregory J. *One Jesus, Many Christs: How Jesus Inspired Not One True Christianity, But Many*. San Francisco: HarperCollins, 1997.

Routley, Erik. *Panorama of Christian Hymnody*. Collegeville, Minn.: Liturgical Press, 1979.

Schauss, Hayyim. *The Jewish Festivals: History and Observance*. Translated by Samuel Jaffe. New York: Schocken Books, 1938.

Scrivener, Frederick Henry Ambrose. *A Plain Introduction to the Criticism of the New Testament for the Use of Biblical Students*. Vol. 1. 4th ed. Edited by Edward Miller. London: George Bell and Sons, 1894.

Scroggs, Robin, and Kent I. Groff. "Baptism in Mark· Dying and Rising with Christ." *Journal of Biblical Literature* 92 (1973): 531-48.

Sfameni Gasparro, Giulia. *Soteriology and Mystic Aspects in the Cult of Cybele and Attis*. Etudes préliminaires aux religions orientales dans l'empire romain 103. Leiden: Brill, 1985.

Skeat, Walter W. *An Etymological Dictionary of the English Language*. New ed., rev. and enlarged. Oxford: Oxford University Press, 1999.

Snyder, Graydon F. *Inculturation of the Jesus Tradition: The Impact of Jesus on Jewish and Roman Cultures*. Harrisburg, Penn.: Trinity Press International, 1999.

Sovik, E. A. *Architecture for Worship*. Minneapolis: Augsburg, 1973.

Taft, Robert F. *The Liturgy of the Hours in East and West: The Origins of the Divine Office and Its Meaning for Today*. Collegeville, Minn.: Liturgical Press, 1986.

Ulansey, David. [A] *The Origins of the Mithraic Mysteries: Cosmology and Salvation in the Ancient World*. New York: Oxford University Press, 1989.

—————. [B] "The Heavenly Veil Torn: Mark's Cosmic 'Inclusio.'" *Journal of Biblical Literature* 110 (1991): 123-25.

White, James F. *Protestant Worship: Traditions in Transition*. Louisville, Ky.: Westminster/John Knox Press, 1989.

White, L. Michael. *Building God's House in the Roman World: Architectural Adaptation among Pagans, Jews, and Christians*. Vol. 1 of *The Social Origins of Christian Architecture*. Harvard Theological Studies. Valley Forge, Penn.: Trinity Press International, 1990.

Wischmeyer, Wolfgang. "Die Aberkiosinschrift als Grabepigramm." *Jahrbuch für Antike und Christentum* 23 (1980): 22-47.

Wright, David F. "The Origins of Infant Baptism—Child Believers' Baptism?" *Scottish Journal of Theology* 40 (1987): 1-23.

Wybrew, Hugh. *The Orthodox Liturgy: The Development of the Eucharistic Liturgy in the Byzantine Rite*. Crestwood, N.Y.: St. Vladimir's Press, 2003.